More praise for *Reclaiming the Sky*

"It is inspiring to see the leadership and courage of so many strong women in this story."

—Denise M. Morrison, President, Campbell U.S.A.,
  Campbell Soup Company

"Murphy provides his reader with a 'road map' for learning from loss that can be applied to any loss in life."

—Gloria Lintermans, author, *The Healing Power of Love: Transcending the Loss of a Spouse to New Love* (with Marilyn Stolzman, Ph.D.)

"We all remember [the events of 9/11] . . . And there are some who carry the memories a bit closer—the families of 9/11 victims, certainly, and workers and witnesses at Ground Zero, but also the thousands upon thousands of airline and airport employees who lost colleagues and friends and not a small bit of innocence one ordinary workday in the fall of 2001.

"The remarkable yet rarely remarked upon thing is that beginning on Sept 13, 2001, and every day since, those same men and women have kept America flying—swallowing whatever fears they may have, dealing with the financial strain of an industry turned upside down and, not least, mourning the end of the romance of flight, which drew many to their aviation careers in the first place.

"Do you ever wonder why they still fly? One man did . . . Tom. Murphy's search to find a common theme in what continued to motivate America's aviation work force turned into a book, *Reclaiming the Sky*."

—from the article "Terrorists Must Never Ground Us" by columnist Virginia Buckingham, *Boston Herald*

RECLAIMING
THE SKY

*9/11 and the Untold Story of the Men
and Women Who Kept America Flying*

TOM MURPHY

AMACOM
American Management Association

NEW YORK | ATLANTA | BRUSSELS | CHICAGO
MEXICO CITY | SAN FRANCISCO | SHANGHAI
TOKYO | TORONTO | WASHINGTON, D.C.

Special discounts on bulk quantities of AMACOM books are available to corporations, professional associations, and other organizations. For details, contact Special Sales Department, AMACOM, a division of American Management Association, 1601 Broadway, New York, NY 10019.
Tel.: 212-903-8316. Fax: 212-903-8083.
Web site: www.amacombooks.org

This publication is designed to provide accurate and authoritative information in regard to the subject matter covered. It is sold with the understanding that the publisher is not engaged in rendering legal, accounting, or other professional service. If legal advice or other expert assistance is required, the services of a competent professional person should be sought.

Library of Congress Cataloging-in-Publication Data

Murphy, Tom (Tom Aloysius), 1949–
    Reclaiming the sky : 9/11 and the untold story of the men and women who kept America flying / by Tom Murphy.
        p. cm.
    ISBN-10: 0-8144-0909-1
    ISBN-13: 978-0-8144-0909-1

    1. September 11 Terrorist Attacks, 2001.   2. Airlines—United States—Employees.   3. Air pilots—United States—Biography.   4. Flight crews—United States—Biography.   I. Title.

HV6432.7.M87 2006
973.931—dc22

                                                        2006016366

Printing number

10 9 8 7 6 5 4 3 2 1

To my wife, Barbara, and my daughter, Caitlin,
great givers both.

Acknowledgments

T HIS BOOK is about community—about the strength of a community and, as such, I want to credit the community that made this book possible.

On the professional side, I wish to thank Sharlene Martin, my agent, who first saw the potential for celebrating aviation employees, and Lisa Wysocky, my editor, whose gift for nuance astounds. I'd like to thank Jacquie Flynn, Executive Editor, and Andy Ambraziejus, Managing Editor, at AMACOM, and their colleagues, including Barbara Chernow, who are spirited as well as talented.

I come from a large family, and I thank them all: my wife, Barbara, and daughter, Caitlin, and my siblings, Larry, Mary Liz, Michael, John, Jimmy, Maura, Peggy, Patti, and Danny, and of course my mom and dad. In addition, I want to thank Elizabeth Connors, Anne Rice Donnelly, Kathleen Rice and Devin Murphy, cousins who read drafts and served in many ways.

And thank you to my friends, who were invaluable to this project —Jeff Pearse, Doug McCormick, Denise Morrison, David Schooler, Jim Reynolds, Dave Westermann, John Westermann, Barrie Brett, Tom Morante, Justin Reed, Peter Monck, Joan Kenney, Mike Mercurio, Curtis Dennis, Jon Clarke, Chuck Robinson, Bob Casey, Lorraine O'Connor, Gerry Ford, Margaret Bishop, John Geddes, Johnny Kelley, Jerry Thon, Jim Miller, and those who were there at the beginning for "Miami Nice" in 1985, including Fr. "Pat," Delia Gorrita, Roy Langer, Seth Bramson, Dave Gergley, Denny Davis, Anna Bustamante, Lisette Manzanares, and Chris DeStefano.

And now to my aviation friends and colleagues.

This is their book. My life would not be so rich without them. You will meet them in the pages that follow, so rather than list all their names here, I'll let you come by them one by one. But there are several who are not in the book, yet who have been wonderful advocates for the goal of this story, which is to support the recovery of aviation employees after 9/11, no matter how long that takes. And so I wish to thank them for their support: Bob Aaronson, Dick Williams, Greg Principato, Bill DcCota, Steve Grossman, Tom Kinton, Bill Sherry, Jim May, Virginia Buckingham, Joanne Holloway, Stephanie Vigilotti, Kathy Crandall and Kathy Ochenrider, aviation leaders who make me proud to be part of this industry.

It's for them that I would like to see any profits from this book go to support aviation charities, including creating an annual award for a top performing aviation charity in the names of Marianne MacFarlane and Jesus Sanchez.

I hope you gain something from this story, a story of ordinary citizens who teach us how to turn tragedy to hope, a story of quiet heroes who keep our country flying.

Contents

Introduction

THE KENNIFER BENCH

I᭙ ᴡᴀs September, 11, 2004, the third anniversary of 9/11.

I sat on a white marble bench called "Kennifer." That's the name Ken and Jennifer Lewis' colleagues at American Airlines had coined for the couple since, as all their friends knew, they were "two peas in a pod." The letters etched on the marble bench stood out boldly in the afternoon sun that filtered through golden leaves: Kᴇɴɴɪꜰᴇʀ. Iɴ Mᴇᴍᴏʀʏ ᴏꜰ Kᴇɴ ᴀɴᴅ Jᴇɴɴɪꜰᴇʀ Lᴇᴡɪs. Sᴇᴘᴛᴇᴍʙᴇʀ 11, 2001. AA/77.

It had taken me a year to find my way to this bench, a memorial Ken and Jennifer's colleagues had created for the couple who had lost their lives on a flight from Washington to Los Angeles on a bright blue day like this one. Life is not a straight line. Living is a series of ups and downs, seemingly random, yet all taking us to a place we need to discover. That's a lesson I learned on my journey to this bench—and to the garden in a small rural Virginia town that housed it. There are no coincidences.

That other morning, three years earlier, my American Airlines Flight 265 had lifted off to the west out of New York's JFK airport, our wing curving north over Manhattan as another American Airlines flight, unseen by me out my window, angled below us on a line for the World Trade Center's North Tower. Time passes, and with it passes the urgency of the questions that seared deep into our souls after 9/11. "Get over it," some say, "Time to move on," say others. But how do we do that?

How do we forgive the unforgivable?

For ten years before the 9/11 attacks, whenever I was in New York, I had worked out of the 65th floor of the World Trade Center's North Tower, headquarters for the Port Authority of New York and New Jersey's aviation division. I'm an aviation trainer. That's been my job since 1986: developing customer service training programs for airports. More than that, it's been my life. An aviation life.

I had come to New York from Boston for a meeting with my Port Authority clients in the North Tower that was scheduled for September 11, 2001. But the meeting was canceled, and I rebooked my flight to head home to Seattle early that Tuesday morning. As I took my seat on the Boeing 757 in Row 25, Seat A, for an 8:20 AM departure out of JFK, I was feeling good—ecstatic in fact. The evening before, a colleague at United Airlines had called to tell me that his bosses in Chicago had approved hiring me to develop a national program for United beginning in January. I sat back, dreaming of January, when I felt a squirming presence in the aisle beside me, and I turned to see a Middle Eastern man—my "nervous guy," as I would come to think of him in the months and years ahead.

He stood in the aisle bouncing up and down on his toes, and my first thought was "what's he doing?" Then I realized he was angling for a better look at the front of the plane. But who does that? I wondered. Who watches people board an airplane from 25 rows back? I tried to make eye contact, but each time I glanced at him, he turned away. He had tiny eyes, the kind that reflect no light, and I thought of the Bob Dylan line, "the vacuum of his eyes." He wore nice clothes, new, given the crisp crease in his slacks, but he didn't seem comfortable in them.

I glanced at my watch. It was 8:10. For the next ten minutes I watched as he continued to crane his neck for a better look at the front of the plane, making it difficult for people to pass. "Give it a rest, buddy. Sit down!" I thought. The morning is too peaceful for your agitation.

"Flight attendants prepare the cabin for departure," the captain said at 8:20. A blond flight attendant stepped forward to close the cabin door, and I turned for another look at my guy—and it was as if all the air had gone out of him. He paused a moment until the flight attendant locked the door, then he turned and walked somewhere to the back of the plane, and I turned to face forward again, thinking of January.

Thank God! I thought, as Seat C remained open beside me.

We all have our memory of the moment we first heard.

"The radar is out in the western United States," the pilot announced over the public address system. We had been in the air about an hour, and I thought, *that's* strange. "We are being diverted to Toronto," he added. "Flight attendants prepare the cabin for landing."

Toronto?

As we pulled to the gate, I reached for my cell phone. I had two messages. One was from my brother who had worked in the World Financial Center across from the World Trade Center until his company had relocated to Long Island during the summer of 2001. He left a message on my line thinking he was calling my wife, "Barbara, I can see the smoke all the way out here," he said. The second message was from my wife. It was succinct. "Call me," she said. "Call me as soon as you get this."

Smoke? What smoke? We had taken off to the west out of JFK, the broad sweep of Manhattan unfolding below us, and I had touched the window, a habit, as I tried to pick out the 65th floor of the North Tower where I imagined my Port Authority colleagues were working at their desks. I had not seen any smoke. Standing in baggage claim in Toronto shortly after 10 AM I tried to get a connection out of Canada when I saw a man with a cell phone to his ear and a stunned look in his eye. "Do you know what's going on?" I asked.

"The Twin Towers."

"Is there smoke or something in New York?"

"Fell," he said.

"What?"

"One just fell," he said, his eyes wide.

"What do you mean fell? Is there damage?" That's as much as my brain could process.

"Fell, as in *fell*," he said, and I remember hearing the words as if there were spaces between each of the letters. A cop appeared, and I walked in the direction the cop pointed, the image of the towers gleaming silver in the sun emblazoned in my brain as I thought: my friends!

What follows is my attempt to regain clarity. Before 9/11 we all came and went, safe in our daily routines. We lived with certain core beliefs unquestioned—safety within our borders included—or at least I did. Then came "After," and with that came "Anger." Anger left unchecked can corrode the soul. This I learned along the way to Kennifer's Bench, though I didn't learn it quickly or easily. Life after all is not a straight line.

We were all attacked on 9/11. Whether we lost loved ones, or simply saw the images on television, the pictures of smoke turning the sky black in New York, Washington, and on a patch of farmland in Shanksville, Pennsylvania, struck all Americans. Our attackers came to drive us apart, to break the connections that bind us, and we kid ourselves if we think the effect of crimes so deliberately committed, as the writer, Anna Quindlen says, "in less time than it takes to read a newspaper," can be put aside without introspection. Healing begins with reflection, not with a time clock that says, "Get over it."

I could not do that, I couldn't "get over it," and so, beginning nearly two years after 9/11, I decided to go back to Newark, Logan, and Dulles airports to talk to my aviation friends and colleagues. These are the three airports in Boston, New York, and Washington that had been used as departure points for the planes that morning; locations where my friends had been directly affected. Many I knew and loved had come into work expecting a routine day, only to find themselves in the middle of a national attack—one in which they had become the *means*. I wanted to talk to them to hear their stories of heartbreak and heroism, but mostly to learn what they were doing to recover—so I too could recover. We've heard the stories of the brave firefighters and police officers, but the heroism of aviation employees that morning—thirty-three aviation employees died that day—has not been as widely reported—until now.

In the following pages you will meet aviation employees who rose up that morning and who continue to rise up. You will meet a group of American Airlines flight attendants who have been devising charity projects, such as the Kennifer garden, to memorialize friends lost on Flight 77. You will meet a mother, an employee at Logan, who put her daughter, a United Airlines customer service agent, on Flight 175 out of Boston that morning. That same afternoon, she went back to the airport to comfort other parents who had lost children. You will meet the general manager of Newark airport. She was nearly killed by falling glass during the first terror attack on the World Trade Center in 1993, but on 9/11 she provided for the safety of fifty thousand travelers as she looked out a window at the terrifying sight of her work-home burning six short miles away.

Mark Hussey, the station manager for United Airlines in Boston, where Flight 175 departed, told me that after 9/11 every day became a tug between "remembering" and "moving on." His point is supported by the World Health Organization, which says that 50 percent of a population recovers quickly after a disaster. Forty percent recovers more slowly, but up to ten percent (or 28 million Americans) can remain anxious long after the event. These are "grapplers," as I call them. I know, because I was one.

As I sat on the Kennifer bench, considering my year-long journey to find this place, not simply the bench, but an understanding of how we learn from loss, I came to realize that once we put our anger aside, the world opens for us again.

Join me if you want to learn from quiet heroes at three airports how to do that. Join me if you want to learn how to move forward again after loss—any loss in your life.

Join me on this journey if you want to learn how to reclaim your sky.

BOOK *One*

THAT DAY

Chapter One
THE GLORY DAYS

MONDAY, September 10, 2001, was more than just a beautiful late summer day on the New Jersey side of the Hudson River; this was a day when many things were going right for Sue Baer, the general manager of Newark International Airport.

In 1994, Sue had achieved a major career goal when she was named general manager of LaGuardia International Airport, thus becoming the first woman to lead a major New York City airport. She was a dynamo, or as one colleague characterized his boss: "Take a lightening bolt, pack it into an attractive five-foot-five inch frame, add blue eyes, sandy hair, a perpetual smile, and an impatience for fools." You get the picture.

By 1996 Sue and her husband, Joe Martella, had a son, Nicky, soon to be followed by the adoption of Elizabeth, from Guatemala. Shortly after that Sue got lucky again: the manager's job at Newark International Airport opened up. Newark was very close to her new home in Montclair, which was good. Newark also had a growing international operation, which was even better, since she loved action. But more than anything, Newark attracted Sue because Newark had history.

In the 1920s, flying was something daredevils did to entertain crowds on Sunday afternoons. Then in 1927, Charles Lindbergh lifted off from Long Island, New York, and 28 hours later, when he touched down in Paris, commercial aviation had been born.

Sensing opportunity, officials from Newark built a runway—the first hard-surfaced runway in the United States. In 1930, Newark introduced the first all-air passenger service to the West Coast. In 1934, Newark built the first central airport administration building, which housed the nation's first airport hotel and restaurant. It combined services such as air traffic control, weather monitoring, and ticketing. An air traffic control tower, also the first in the country, sat atop the new building and used colored lights to signal planes: red to stay aloft, green to land. It was the dawn of the glory days.

In many ways Newark pioneered aviation in America, and Sue wanted to restore those days of glory. One day, Paul Wood, a Port Authority redevelopment official, came to Sue with an idea that would help her with her plan. (In both Boston and New York, airports are divisions of their port authorities, which also operate bridges, tunnels, and ports in those areas. The Port Authority of New York and New Jersey, and Massport, the Massachusetts Port Authority in Boston, make money from their bridges, tunnels, and seaports, but the landing fees the airports charge the airlines bring in most of the revenue.)

Because Newark's original terminal building sat in the path of the airport's expansion, no one could use the building, but they could not tear it down either because it was a national "historic landmark." Paul's idea was to move the building, fix it up, and have it become the aviation department's headquarters.

"Perfect!" Sue exclaimed, sensing the opportunity to link the future with aviation's storied past.

On Monday, September 10, Sue wrapped up a progress meeting on the renovation of the old building. The work was moving toward completion.

While others went to lunch, she dashed to the mall to pick up clothes for five-year-old Nicky, who had begun kindergarten that week. Sue drove quickly to complete her errands and get back before her staff finished lunch. People accepted that about Sue, that she was a multitasker. Given a choice between food and action, it was no contest. A bargain hunter, she passed up and down the aisles at the outlet mall, grabbing items for Nicky and Elizabeth, along with a pair of shoes for herself. But as she stood at the checkout counter waiting for the cashier to total her purchases, her beeper went off. She called in. It was John Jacoby, her second in command at the airport.

"We got a fire," he said.

"Fire? What fire?"

"In the old administration building."

"What!"

"The roof is burning."

How could that be? She had just passed the building! Sue paid quickly and sprinted to her car, while calling the operations desk to ask, "Anyone hurt?"

"No," said the duty manager.

"I'm on my way."

As she approached, smoke arched over Runway 22R, the airport's main runway, and she called the duty manager again to make sure Port Authority staff had coordinated with the control tower to close the airport. That was something no one liked to do, close the airport—it cost so much. But the Port Authority fire department had been assigned to fight the construction fire and that precluded the firefighters being available for their regular duty, which was to stand by for aircraft emergencies. As a result, the airport had to be shut down. Sue wanted to make sure her people coordinated with the FAA (Federal Aviation Administration) to make the shut down as "tight" as possible, to spare passengers aggravation as well as to save costs. Then she called Bill DeCota, her boss at the World Trade Center, to apprise him.

It wasn't unusual for Sue and her boss to be in different buildings. The Port Authority of New York and New Jersey owned the World Trade Center, and the aviation division had its offices in the World Trade Center on the 65th floor of the North Tower. Many of the Port Authority workers at each airport had at one time done rotations in the tall building, which is why the Port Authority workers at Newark knew so many people in the World Trade Center personally, and why recovering from 9/11 was so hard.

As Sue said, "We lost our home."

For several hours, late into the afternoon, Sue worked with fire officials. By early evening things had more or less returned to normal, preparations had been made to reopen the airport, and Sue focused on what the fire would do to upset the already tight reconstruction schedule on the old building.

At about this same time, in the lobby of the Newark Airport Marriott, the airport's on-site hotel, a trim Middle Eastern man, Ziad Jarrah, checked in. Several days earlier the lean, 26-year-old Jarrah had checked out of the Panther Motel, a nondescript economy motel in Deerfield Beach, Florida, where he and two colleagues had put the final touches on their plans for a "mission," as Jarrah called it.

Jarrah had spent ten days at the Florida motel with Mohammed Atta and Marwan Al-Shehhi, his apartment roommates back in Hamburg, Germany, where they had resided in the late 1990s. Atta and Al-Shehhi focused on two flights they planned to take out of Boston to Los Angeles on September 11, while Jarrah made flight arrangements for a trip out of Newark to San Francisco. The three men, part of a four-man leadership team assigned to the "mission," worked from an Internet connection linked to the phone line in the manager's office at the beachside Panther Motel, a concession Jarrah had extracted from the manager by schmoozing him.

By Monday afternoon, September 10th, Jarrah stood at the front desk of the Newark Airport Marriott with broad shoulders toned up from a series of sessions at a Florida body-building parlor that summer. Behind him, three Middle Eastern men, all with pensive expressions, waited against a felt rope. Jarrah did not know the men very well. Certainly he had not known them long. They were Saudis—all in their twenties—and had trained in Al Qaeda camps in Afghanistan. Wiry and expressionless, silent types, they were known only to Jarrah as "muscle men"—appointees assigned to him for his task, as others had been assigned to Atta and Al-Shehhi, and a fourth member of their team, Hani Hanjour, who had been tapped to take a flight out of Washington, DC.

One of the Saudis, Saeed Alghandi, twenty-five, had a narrow face and pointed ears. He stood with his head cocked to the side as he watched Jarrah deal with the Marriott desk clerk in his patented, breezy manner, which was perfected, so as to disarm. Ahmed Alnami, twenty-three, had thick hair and wore a melancholy expression, like the dreamy gaze that singers in boy bands affect, but the turned-down corners of his mouth gave his face a vicious stamp. The third Saudi, Al Haznawi, twenty, was the hair-trigger one in the bunch. Eyes black as coal lumps, he stared straight ahead. Several weeks earlier he had made a "video will." According to John Miller, in his book, *The Cell,* in the taped video will Haznawi said he planned to attack America and send a "bloodied message" to the world.

Jarrah paid cash and the group walked across the polished floor to the gleaming elevators that took them upstairs to the third floor. In a curious move, Jarrah ordered seven rooms for the four of them for the night, requesting rooms that faced east and also looked back across the runways, with a view of the New York Harbor and the skyline of lower Manhattan.

That skyline rose against a deepening sky in the east, as the salmon-colored sunset splashed across the western sky, and the sun itself, a fine-edged persimmon ball, set in the hotel parking lot behind them. The group said prayers from a manual that had been prepared for them, as Jarrah checked on their flights in the morning. He was concerned about the building fire at Newark, but he was told everything would be back to normal by that evening. His early morning flight, United Flight 93, nonstop to San Francisco, was on schedule and would depart at 8:00 AM. This pleased Jarrah.

As Sue Baer inched along in northbound traffic, an audio P.D. James novel playing to help settle her mind, Jarrah called to make reservations for dinner in the airport restaurant. There were four restaurants, and he asked which one was the best. He had an extra $700 in his pocket, wired to him by his unsuspecting family in Lebanon. Jarrah had told his family he needed an addition to the allowance they regularly sent, saying he wanted it for "fun," and as usual, his father indulged him without question.

The hostess gave him the name of the priciest restaurant, Priscilla's. It was small and dimly lit, but a tall, sparkling chandelier hung in the center of the room, giving the dining area a soft, elegant glow.

Jarrah requested a table for four. The hostess made the reservation, and that night, September 10, as Sue Baer tucked Nicky and Elizabeth into bed and 3,023 other unsuspecting souls performed their routines and duties from Boston to Washington, DC, the four sets of team leaders and their assorted "muscle men"—including Jarrah's group at Newark—made their final preparations.

As the night deepened, Jarrah and his three expressionless colleagues took the elevator down. They crossed the marbled lobby and entered the hotel's fanciest restaurant, where the hostess greeted them with a smile. She sat them in the main room where they dined on steak, courtesy of Jarrah's extra allowance from his family. Jarrah and his troops ate in silence that evening, surrounded by the soft, elegant glow of Priscilla's chandelier, a symbol of the airport's glory days.

Chapter Two
SUE

SUE BAER coaxed her son Nicky out of the car in front of his kindergarten in Montclair, New Jersey, the next morning. It was Tuesday, September 11, senior staff meeting day at Newark International Airport, and though she didn't know how it had become the airport general manager's job to bring bagels, nevertheless she had brought a bag along.

"I want to go to work with you," said Nicky, clutching the warm bag as he stood in front of the car door. For his part, the boy was considered an airport expert by Port Authority staff at Newark. One day that summer he had distinguished himself at a firehouse "Kid's Day." In response to a question about the color of the engines, Nicky had sprung to his feet and announced to all the other kids that airport fire engines were yellow instead of red because yellow was easier to see at night.

"First you go to school, work hard, get a college degree. Then you can come to work with mommy," Sue said. "You can take my job. Now give me the bagels."

The boy relented and by 8 AM on that bright Indian summer morning, Sue had swung her maroon '99 Chevy Impala back onto the highway. She proceeded south toward Newark International, but as traffic slowed, Sue slipped the next tape from the P.D. James novel into the player, and therefore was not listening to the radio when shortly before nine she turned into the airport drive that led to her office in Building 10, the airport administration building, and saw a wisp of black smoke in the distance.

As Sue made her way past Continental's Terminal C, the smoke looked like a tiny cloud, but fires sprouted in buildings along the water in Jersey City all the time, so she didn't think much about it. Instead, while she continued to watch the smoke on the horizon, she did a mental inventory of senior staff issues, including the rescheduling required for Port Authority staff who had helped fight the fire on Monday. But when she turned another corner, suddenly it occurred to her that maybe this wasn't a fire in Jersey City after all. This looked, though that was impossible, like it was coming from the World Trade Center, directly across New York Harbor from Newark International.

"We have a report that a small plane has hit the World Trade Center," said a newscaster as she turned on the radio.

"Oh, my God!" she breathed, as she stared at the cloud of smoke.

If this was true and a small plane had gone off course and hit the twin towers, it most likely would have come out of Teterboro, a general aviation facility ten miles north. Though much smaller, Teterboro was her responsibility along with Newark International, and she realized she might own this event—whatever it was. Sue jammed her car into her parking space and zoomed into the building. She hurried past the police desk, as several police offiers, all friends, began gathering up their things.

"What's the report?" she shouted through the glass.

One of the sergeants replied, "World Trade's been hit. Small plane, they say. We're mobilizing to go over."

That was customary policy, whenever an incident occurred at one Port Authority facility (the World Trade Center was owned by the Port Authority) staff from other Port Authority facilities, including JFK, LaGuardia, Newark, the bus terminal, and several bridges, tunnels, and seaports, would rush to provide support.

Sue's office was on the third floor, but rather than wait for the elevator, she ran up the stairs. Once she arrived, she handed the bag of bagels to people milling about and said, "Staff meeting's cancelled. I'll be on the fourth floor in operations."

And up she went, taking the stairs two at a time. The fourth floor operations room, a cramped space jammed with computers, offered a straight-shot view across the flatlands of New Jersey to New York and lower Manhattan, six nautical miles away. The operations department, familiarly called "Ops" by airport and Port Authority staff, oversees the day-to-day operations at an airport, including the various service companies, such as concessions, and ground transportation, to ensure the airport runs smoothly. As operations was divided into three parts—airside (from the terminals to the perimeter gates, including the runways), terminals (everything inside the terminals), and landside (everything from the terminals to the highways leading into the airport, including the front drives and the parking garages)—this budding tragedy would use every one of their available resources.

As Sue arrived, Frank Loprano, the airport's slender, meticulous, airside manager, was working the phones, trying to get more information from the control tower.

"Where did that plane come from?" Sue asked, then when no reply was forthcoming, repeated with more intensity, "*Where did that plane come from?*"

As John Jacoby, Sue's calm, studied, manager of airport services arrived, Sue was on the phone to Teterboro, but officials there said they had no record of a small plane hitting anything.

It was now 9:02.

John got on the phones, and began making contact with Port Authority departments at the airport, including landside, maintenance, and terminals, to mobilize them. In a corner of the room, Trevor Liddle, head of maintenance, spoke in a measured English accent on a cell phone.

"Trevor, what is it?" Sue asked, as she watched his face fall. Across New York Harbor the World Trade Center's North Tower emitted an expanding comma of black smoke high into the air, the smoke curving toward Brooklyn.

"It's Laurie," he said, meaning his wife.

"What about Laurie?"

"She's in there. She's in the North Tower. On the 83rd floor."

Across the flats, Sue could see smoke pouring from the top floors of the North Tower. "Trevor, you talk to her, you tell her to get out of there," she said, thinking that some crazy pilot had made a mistake, some crazy pilot had messed up and flown off course. Then to Loprano: "Get me JFK. See if they know anything about what's going on."

It was 9:03 AM.

Suddenly, in full view, a silver flash angled above New York Harbor, glided over Battery Park, and slammed into the South Tower, sending a bright orange glow into the underside of the black smoke.

"What was that?" everyone shouted.

"Was that a plane?" Sue asked. "Did we just see a plane or is that more smoke coming out of the North Tower?"

"That was a plane," said John. "Hitting Tower Two."

"Yes," said Frank Loprano. "A second plane."

"Then this is no accident," she said. Al Graser, the general manager of Kennedy, came on the phone, but she asked him to hold a moment. "Shut the airport down," she told Frank.

"But I've got a plane about to take off on 22R," he said.

"I don't give a damn. Shut it down," said Sue instinctively, without a second thought for second guessers who might point out that a decision like that could cost upward of a million dollars. "This is no accident! Shut the damn airport down!"

She turned her attention to Al on the phone. "Somebody's attacking us," she said. She urged him to shut his airport down. He did. Then she got LaGuardia on the phone and spoke to Warren Kroeppel, the general manager.

"We're being attacked, Warren," she said. "Shut your airport down."

He did also.

Nineteen men came to overtake four airplanes. Atta and his team of four "muscle men" departed Boston on American Airlines Flight 11 at 7:59 AM. Contact was lost with the plane over Gardiner, Massachusetts, at 8:14.

United Airlines Flight 175, with Al-Shehhi and four of his team aboard, lifted off from Boston at 8:14. Contact was lost over the same stretch of low mountains in western Massachusetts twenty-nine minutes later at 8:43.

American Airlines Flight 77, with Hani Hanjour and a team of four, departed Dulles International in Washington, DC, at 8:20. Contact was lost at 8:56 over western Virginia.

A fourth plane, United Flight 93, which carried Jarrah and his group, departed Newark at 8:40. It plied the skies over Pennsylvania as Sue Baer spoke rapid fire to the airport's control tower.

The four men who led teams on each of the planes had begun their journey in Hamburg, Germany, three years earlier, according to *The Cell: Inside the 9/11 Plot and Why the FBI and CIA Failed to Stop It* by Johny Miller and Michael Stone, with Chris Mitchell. Atta, the group's leader, had rented an apartment in a bland, nondescript section of the city at 54 Marienstrasse in October 1998 as a base for their operations. He and a corenter on the lease, Ramsi Binalshibb, invited other young Muslims who wished to withdraw from the mostly blond Germans who surrounded them at the engineering school they attended to join them. On his bank slips, Atta gave a clue as to his intentions for the apartment. "The House of Followers," he called the place.

Over the next two years and more, the drab apartment at 54 Marienstrasse would play host to twenty-nine "followers," acolytes who subscribed to the goal of creating "caliphate," the dream of a radical Islamic state that would impose its Islamic fundamentalism on the world. As part of their training, Atta led the followers to Al Qaeda training camps in Afghanistan, but it was not a straight line from 54

Marienstrasse to the Afghan camps for these devout young men. First, there was the Al Quds Mosque in Hamburg, where the group took their prayers and sharpened their idealism. With their prayers, they received direction from a host of imans who encouraged them to see Allah as a fiery, recriminating god and to see America as an enemy.

After Friday night prayers the men would retire to a dim Hamburg cafe where they would discuss the imans' lectures and accelerate their fervor. Then they would take their passion for jihad against America back to 54 Marienstrasse where they would continue their discussions about tactics late into the night. Their plan was fluid, always evolving, but always it involved Boeing airliners—757s and 767s.

"What's going on?" Sue Baer shouted, as she peered across the tarmac at the FAA tower with twin plumes of smoke rising from the New York skyline beyond.

"We don't know," came the answer.

"Who is doing this?"

"We don't know."

"For God's sakes, are there any more planes out there?"

"We don't know," came the repeated response.

Two hours earlier on that Tuesday morning, Jarrah and the "muscle men" on his team had stepped out the front door of the Newark Airport Marriott. They had stood in the slanting light of the new day, their muscles rippling under their suits, as they waited with other travelers under the hotel's covered porch for the shuttle. When the red-and-white shuttle bus pulled up, the four stepped aboard, mixing quietly with the other travelers and rocking in rhythm with the turns as the bus made its way to P-4, the terminus for the Air Train monorail to the airport terminals.

"Terminal traffic to the left. The first stop is Terminal C, then B, then A," said the red coat on the Air Train platform. The Red Coats are the familiar name given to security agents who are employed by Gateway Security, a contractor at Port Authority airports. At Newark, they work on the Air Train system as customer service agents, providing directions and offering other assistance as needed.

Gateway Security operates with instructions from Sue Baer to invoke a "Five- and Ten-Foot Rule." The moment a traveler comes within ten feet, the red coat is obliged to step forward and make eye contact. At five feet, the agent is required to engage the customer. I know, because that was my job at Newark, given to me by Sue beginning in 1990, to teach them how.

When the next train pulled into the station that morning, Jarrah and his group stepped aboard. They didn't need directions. Together with Atta, Al-Shehhi, and Hanjour, Jarrah had practiced his deception, as the others had practiced at their assigned airports, passing unnoticed among those they intended to destroy.

At the final terminal stop, Terminal A, the four descended the escalator. They walked past the potted plants and the food court, with Treat Street and Famiglia Caffe on the left, and Jersey!, a souvenir shop, to the right. At the entrance to United gates 10 through 18, they put their carry-on luggage on the belt where security screeners, employees of a private security company, directed them through the metal detectors.

At Gate 17, the four approached the United Airlines gate agent. The agent, a long-time employee, accepted their boarding passes, which he slipped into the computer, called an Electronic Gate Register, or EGR, then returned the stubs to the silent, sullen men, pausing a moment before he handed Jarrah his pass.

In the minutes before 8 AM, Jarrah and his colleagues walked down the jetway ramp to United Flight 93. The plane, a Boeing 757 with 37 seven passengers and a crew of seven, prepared to push back for an on-time departure to San Francisco. As he sat in seat 1B, the first row in first class, Jarrah made a cell phone call to Ayel Senguen, his girlfriend in Germany. When she didn't answer, he left a message on her answering machine, telling her that he would see her September 22 for a family wedding in Lebanon. Then he clicked the phone shut. Even at this late hour this self-professed religious man apparently had not stopped lying to the person closest to him.

The plane pushed back from Gate 17 on time. Newark air traffic had been especially heavy that morning, and Flight 93 sat in queue on the tarmac, its engines running. It didn't get off the ground until 8:40, but now, as the minutes ticked past nine o'clock and Sue appealed for more information from FAA officials in the tower, Flight 93 settled into its cruising altitude above Pennsylvania.

At 9:25, flight attendants undid their seatbelts and prepared beverages in the galleys, while controllers on the ground in Cleveland received a greeting from the pilot.

"Good-morning," said the pilot, Jason Dahl, brightly, but three minutes later, at 9:28—twenty-five minutes after the second plane struck the World Trade Center, Cleveland heard signs of a struggle aboard Flight 93, then a pause. Following the pause, a voice broke the silence and Cleveland controllers heard a man, most likely Ziad Jarrah, address the passengers over the public address with bated breath and in broken English.

"Ladies and gentlemen," he said. "This is the captain. Please sit down. Keep remaining sitting. We have a bomb aboard."

Chapter Three
MARIANNE AND JESUS

It had been hot and humid in Boston during the summer of 2001—and even stuffier yet in the windowless media room at Logan International Airport where I held customer service training classes for United Airlines staff. Mark Hussey and Steve Bolognese, managers for United at Logan, had asked me to help prepare their people for the rigors of an aviation summer.

I liked Mark and Steve. Mark was a bottom line guy. He talked about "business," but often peppered his speeches with the words "my people," and in training sessions he backed that up by taking a front row seat. Steve talked about "my people," and occasionally I heard the word, "business." As a team, they worked together perfectly.

The summer before 2001, United had experienced labor unrest. That unrest, combined with nasty weather in the midwest during much of the summer of 2000, created havoc for travelers and increased stresses for United's customer service agents who had to deal with the cranky customers. Hoping to avoid a repeat of the mayhem, or at least fortify their staff in advance of the summer, Mark and Steve had asked me to tailor my "Airport Ambassador" program to prepare their front line staff.

One morning in June 2001, a curly-haired young woman poked

her head into the empty media room as I set papers down in front of vacant chairs.

"No one here yet?" she asked, as she looked at her watch. Then she went to one of the phones on the wall and made a call. "They're downstairs working a delayed flight," she said after hanging up. "Let me see if I can help them so they can get up here."

I formed three impressions of Marianne MacFarlane that morning: First, the curly hair. Second, the no-nonsense way she went to the phone and made the call; here was a lady of action. But third, most important, the way she thought of her colleagues in a time of stress.

Later that month, I had Jesus Sanchez in class. He was a big, affable young man with dark, round eyes and an infectious smile. I called him up for a role play and gave him the assignment of acting like an agitated agent faced with an aggressive customer. Like a hooked fish that doesn't want to come into the boat, he balked.

"Come on, you can do it," I said. But each time I introduced the "customer" into the scene and said, "Go," Jesus continued to blush. Try as I might to get him to act sourly, he still spoke to the "customer" in a soothing, considerate tone.

"Better get someone else for your skit," a voice called out from the back of the room. "It's impossible for Jesus to be mean." Jesus turned and bowed to the group, then gave me a nod, grateful for the reprieve as I allowed him to return to his seat.

On the afternoon of 9/11, as confusion reigned and the press bombarded Massport officials with demands for information, John Duval, the Director of Aviation Operations, and Ed Freni, the Deputy Director of Aviation Operations, spoke to the press in the media room. They told what they knew—which wasn't much at that point—but they did have one item. Two passengers on United Flight 175, the second plane to strike the World Trade Center in New York, had been United Airlines employees at Logan: Marianne MacFarlane and Jesus Sanchez.

Reporters wrote in their pads and TV cameras rolled as John and Ed stood in the same spot in the media room where Marianne had been helpful, and where Jesus had stood beside me, refusing "to be mean."

On the morning of September 11, just north of Logan, it was 3:55 AM and still dark on a quiet street in Revere, Massachusetts, where Anne MacFarlane awoke before her alarm. This was Anne's routine, to rise in the predawn darkness in the same row house on the same huddled street where she and her late husband, a lifelong employee at a General Electric paint factory, had raised their family. She did it for Marianne, her daughter and "best friend."

Marianne had moved home to live with her mom five years earlier, after Anne's husband had passed away. One day, several days after her father's funeral, Marianne had called Anne from the airport in Bangor, Maine, where Marianne worked as the station manager for US Air Express, a commuter airline.

"Mom," she said. "I'm coming home."

"Great," said Anne. "What flight are you on?"

Logan Airport was but minutes away from Revere and Anne grabbed a pen to jot down her daughter's flight number.

But Marianne said, "No, Mom. I mean I'm coming home. I've got a U-Haul packed, and I'm moving home to live with you."

They had always been close, Anne and Marianne. And like "best friends," they looked out for one another. This morning, Marianne had to be at work at United Airlines at 4:30 AM to check in for her job as a customer service agent, the job she had taken—along with a pay cut—after moving home from Bangor. Marianne could have driven to work, but that would have necessitated getting up at 3:30, parking the car in Chelsea, and riding the employee bus. One day Anne suggested to Marianne that she let her drive her to work, to save Marianne some sleep time. As so often happens, one day led to another, and so this had become Anne's routine, to rise moments before her daughter's alarm, in anticipation of it.

Ringgggg, went the alarm in Marianne's upstairs room that morning. Marianne intended to go into work that day, but only until 7:30 AM. Then she planned to catch a plane—she had flying privileges—and fly to Los Angeles. It had been a busy summer at Logan and now that September had arrived and things had slowed down, Marianne and a group of colleagues had made plans to grab a break. Several friends had gone out to Las Vegas the previous Saturday, but Marianne planned to grab Flight 175 to the "City of Angels." There she would switch to a plane that would take her to Las Vegas.

No problem, she told the group that had gone out ahead. "I want to get a couple more days of work in, then I'll fly out on Tuesday with Jesus."

Jesus Sanchez and Marianne had it all arranged: Marianne would put in a few hours in the customer service booth Tuesday morning, then go to the gate and help board Flight 175, a nonstop to Los Angeles, before Jesus arrived. Then, together, they would get on the plane. Marianne was thorough and methodical; she had their tickets printed ahead of time: first class, seats 1A and B.

"Marianne! Your alarm is ringing!" called Anne from the bottom of the stairs, still dressed in her housecoat.

"Yeah, yeah, yeah," Marianne called back, part of their ritual. Downstairs, Anne made coffee and toast, while Rexie, the dog Marianne had gotten from the pound as a guard for her sick grandmother, watched her eat. Marianne's grandmother had lived next door until she passed away, then Rexie had become Marianne's dog. Now she slipped a toast crust under the table to the dog, another part of the ritual, and Rexie chomped away.

Anne got the keys to start the car and moments later mother and daughter rode silently the seven minutes it took to pull up to Terminal C. It was now 4:29 AM, a minute before Marianne was scheduled to punch in. She moved quickly, gathering her things, including the suitcase she had packed for her trip to Las Vegas, but then she broke the ritual.

"Good-bye, Mom," she said.

Anne turned to stare at her daughter. She watched as Marianne, red curls flapping, scampered into the terminal and waved one more time, with a flourish, before turning and scooting away.

"Good-bye?" Anne wanted to call after her.

The comment had caught Anne by surprise. All the mornings she had driven Marianne to work, not one morning in three years had her daughter ever said "Good-bye."

Maybe "See ya," or "So long."

But never "good-bye."

Chapter Four
JOHN

The morning of September 11, Mohammed Atta sat in seat 8B at the front of the plane in Boston waiting for Flight 11 to push back from Gate 32 in Terminal B.

Several days earlier, he had come north from Florida's Panther Motel where he had spent time making final preparations. Together with his flaccidly agreeable cousin, Marwan Al-Shehhi, and a Lebanese-born aviation enthusiast, Ziad Jarrah, Atta had made travel reservations from his room, and wired left-over money back to associates in the Middle East. Then he had cleaned out the room and dropped a bag in the dumpster out back. The bag included a Koran and a Boeing 767 flight manual. Now, on this bright, blue morning, he sat beside A. Aloumari, a Saudi who had been assigned to him. When his cell phone rang, it was Al-Shehhi calling from less than three hundred yards away.

The night before, Al-Shehhi had taken a room in Boston. The four men accompanying him were from Saudi Arabia. One of the Saudis had called an escort service to ask for a prostitute who would come over and have sex with four men, but when he was given the price, $400, he said it was too high. On the morning of September 11, Al-Shehhi checked in at the United counter with two of the men in his group. The agent, who had taken Steve Bolognese's and my customer service class that summer, posed the required security questions to Al-Shehhi and the two men, including, "Have you packed your bags yourself? Have you left your bags unattended at any time?"

They were standard questions, but the two men with Al-Shehhi could not understand her. Smiling, she repeated herself. Still the two Saudis had difficulty understanding her until Al-Shehhi, ever the unctuous intermediary, stepped forward to help. The two men finally answered the questions. "Yes, we have packed our own bags. No, we have not left our bags unattended at any time." Then the trio passed through security screening without incident before Al-Shehhi called Atta from a pay phone on the United concourse in Terminal C.

Whatever they talked about, it was quick, because nineteen minutes later Al-Shehhi boarded United Flight 175 at Gate 19 and took a seat in the second row. He slid in behind Marianne MacFarlane and Jesus Sanchez, who sat together in seats 1A and 1B.

American Flight 11 lifted off from Logan at 7:59 AM, with Atta and his group. A short interval later, at 8:14, United 175, took off along the same path with Al-Shehhi and his group.

In Newark, several hundred miles south, Jarrah accepted his boarding pass stub from the agent at United Airlines Gate 17 before walking down the jetway to Flight 93.

In Washington, DC, American Airlines Flight 77, nonstop from Dulles to Los Angeles, prepared for an 8:10 departure at Gate D-26. The pilot, Charles Burlingame, who had flown in from Los Angeles the evening before, performed his cross-checks. This included getting out tiny paintbrushes to dust the controls. Burlingame was a stickler for safety, but he was also adamant about time. He wanted to get his plane up and out, and he would.

At 8:20, Flight 77 angled out over Virginia and the green fields below. The "data" of external fact was set; the dominos were arranged in place.

Aviation and America's longest day was about to begin.

Not long after Anne MacFarlane dropped Marianne off at Terminal C at Logan International Airport, a navy blue Ford Explorer passed through Revere going the other way in the dark. Inside the Massport-issued car, John Duval, the airport's deputy director of operations, navigated the final turns through back streets into work. This was his routine, developed long ago when he began working for Massport as a teenager, pushing a broom in the parking garage. John had harbored ambitions, even then, and he had long ago discovered his secret for success: come early and stay late.

Each morning John, a ringer for MSNBC's *Hardball* host Chris Mathews, rose at 4 AM, grabbed a bagel and large coffee from the greasy spoon around the corner from his house in Beverly, made the hour-long drive south into Boston, and arrived at his desk an hour before others in the executive aviation office arrived.

It was good policy for a guy committed to rising to the top, but the approach also gave him a fighting chance to put a dent in the pile of paper—including the myriad reports that required responses—that is the life of an operations director at a busy U.S. airport.

John had a fun side too, which I knew well. Several years earlier he had taken six months of evenings after work to build a garage next to his house. The garage had nothing to do with cars. It was all about the upstairs, where John created an elaborate game room. It had a state-of-the-art sound system with every Sheryl Crow record available, and a pool table. I spent a night at his house one time, and I saw him in action: he would invite station managers from Logan's various airlines to his "garage." Over pool or poker or whatever, they would solve intractable problems that had resisted solution at work. The guy was a genius.

Forty-eight years old and determined to eat better and work back into shape (if he ever found the time), John had grown up in Winthrop, a small peninsula that juts out like a sandy spit into Massachusetts Bay. It is just a few hundred yards from Boston Harbor and less than a mile from the northernmost runway at Logan. As a boy, he would ride his bike to the edge of Winthrop and watch the planes land. At the time, John thought he wanted to be a harbor captain like his grandfather. A harbor captain was a guy who rowed a boat out to big ocean liners waiting to enter Boston Harbor.

"No kidding," John said, "my grandfather would row his boat, then would climb a rope ladder and board the ship. There, he would take control of the ocean liner from the ship's captain and navigate the vessel the mile or so into the docks. My grandfather had arms like Arnold Schwarzenegger. Big, huge arms, and I wanted to be just like him."

John's grandfather had grown up in Newfoundland, one of fourteen boys. "All of the boys were named Joseph," said John. "There were two girls in the family. Both were named Mary."

The old harbor captain took a shine to his young grandson and he created a game to inspire the boy. "He would give me a penny for every push up I could do," Duval said. "First, I would do ten. Then twenty. Soon I was up to a hundred. That was a lot of money for a kid in those days, a dollar."

The push-up thing got John into trouble, however. One day when he was a freshman in high school, the gym teacher called for everyone to drop to the floor and do push ups. After an interval the teacher blew his whistle and went around the room asking kids to count off how many they had done.

"One kid said six. Another ten," Duval said. "But when he came to me, I said 'a hundred.' "

The gym teacher set his clipboard aside. "Oh, yeah? Come up here." John did. The gym teacher pointed to the floor and said, "Show me." John dropped down and reeled off another hundred perfect push ups.

"Okay," the gym teacher said. "Back to your spot, son. As you were."

John Duval sat at his desk the morning of September 11. Above all else, John is a detail guy. I saw that clearly the day I met him. I was interviewing to offer my "Airport Ambassador" training program for Massport at Logan, and he assembled staff from a dozen different departments to quiz me. I liked that about him, how precise he was. He was an "Ops" guy. He didn't like surprises.

As the sun climbed in the cobalt sky and planes changed places at gates behind him, John culled through a mountain of papers, reviewing airside maintenance reports, answering FAA mail, and checking off things he wanted his duty managers to do that day. When his phone rang, it was his son, Michael, calling from his job at a used car lot in Peabody, half an hour north of Boston.

"Hi, Michael. What's up?"

"Did you hear the news? A plane just hit the World Trade Center in New York."

"Hit what?"

"Turn on the TV, Dad."

"Thanks," John said, and he reached for the clicker, but the phone rang again. It was one of his duty managers.

"John, something bad's happening."

"What's going on?"

"I just hung up with the tower. They say a plane hit the World Trade Center. Another one is missing."

"Missing?"

"They think the two planes came from here."

"I'll call Ed," said John.

If an actor wanted to prepare for an acting role as an airport official, he'd study Ed Freni. For twenty-seven years, Ed, a kinetic bundle of energy with a thick George Clooney-like shock of hair, had worked at Logan. Twenty-five of those years were with American Airlines. In high school and college he had been a hockey player. He played because he loved the competition, the hard skate-and-check-against-the-boards part of the game. That's what had attracted him to aviation—the competitive nature of the business.

But he was accessible as well, and generous. When he was the station manager for American Airlines in Boston and I needed prizes for the Airport Ambassador incentive, I'd always go to Ed. Getting free air tickets for charity causes is not an easy task. But Ed always took my call. "Whad'ya need?" he'd ask, year after year.

"Two to the Caribbean. Two to New York. A set to the West Coast."

"You got 'em," he'd say. To me, that was Ed Freni, "Mr. You Got 'Em."

In 1999, Ed took a position as Logan's Director of Operations, second to Tom Kinton, Massport's long-time airport manager. Ed hit it off famously with fellow Massport employee John Duval. The two quickly became as close as brothers, and so on the morning of 9/11 it was a given that John Duval would call Ed Freni.

———————

The morning of September 11, Ed was at an on-site seminar, which ironically was called "How to Deliver Bad News." He had just finished a call with Tom Kinton in Montreal where Tom was attending a meeting when his phone rang again, minutes before nine.

"Ed, something's up," said John. "A plane crashed into the World Trade Center this morning."

"What?" Ed walked to a corner of the room in the Logan Office Center, out of earshot from the other seminar participants. This was impossible. Massport had never been given any warnings.

"They think it might have come from here."

"A plane hit the World Trade Center?"

"Yeah, and there's another one missing. They think that one might have come from here, too."

"Whose planes are they?"

"Don't know. But you better get over here."

"Where are you?"

"I'm on my way up to the (FAA control) tower. Eighteenth floor."

"Give me five minutes."

Ed Freni hung up and clapped his cell phone shut. For twenty-seven years he had worked for an airline. A call like that had always terrified him.

———————

As he hurried down the stairs, Ed shifted into operational mode. It was second nature. His first thought was to call the American station in Terminal B. His antenna picked up concern in the office. They were worried about Flight 11, the 7:45 nonstop to Los Angeles.

"Amy Sweeney called from the air," he was told by a friend. Amy, one of six flight attendants on Flight 11, had been part of Ed's crew when he had been the in-flight supervisor.

"What did she say?" he asked.

"She said they were flying over Manhattan."

"Manhattan? Eleven's a flight to Los Angeles."

"Amy said they were flying low, then her line went dead."

It was instinctive again, but as Ed spoke on his cell phone on his way up to the Massport aviation office on the sixteenth floor of the FAA tower, he asked for the manifest—the "dec system"—which holds names of passengers on a flight by seat number. In the event of an accident, the deck system is purged so officials can begin contacting next of kin.

Ed asked friends at American to fax him a copy of the manifest for Flight 11. It was a hunch, the kind that comes with twenty-seven years experience. It was 9:05 AM when the elevator doors opened and Ed reached the eighteenth floor. In a corner of the conference room, John Duval spoke on the phone and signaled toward the television.

"Look!"

On the screen, a silver sliver angled across lower Manhattan and slammed into the South Tower of the World Trade Center. "Oh, my God!" Ed cried.

"While you were on your way up," said John. "Just happened."

Again, Ed watched as the television replay showed a second plane hitting the World Trade Center. Ed stared at the twin columns of black smoke darkening the Manhattan skyline, his mouth agape. "This is an attack," he said. "The country's being attacked. You know for sure they came from here?"

"That's what I'm trying to find out from the boys upstairs."

While John spoke with FAA officials on one line, two floors above them in the tower, Ed called his contacts at various airlines at Logan. He had the conversation with Amy Sweeney at American as one lead, now he learned that United was also experiencing a problem.

He asked his friends at United to pull the manifest for the flight they worried about, Flight 175, nonstop to Los Angeles. It had fifty-six passengers on board and a crew of nine. Airlines are hesitant to declare that one of their planes has been involved in an accident. It's not something officials are quick to do, but again Ed had a hunch. He asked United to fax him their manifest for Flight 175, while John Duval continued to work the phones with the FAA.

"What do you know up there?" John asked the tower.

"United 175 came from here. We lost contact at 8:43."

"Any more out there?"

"We're not getting a response from Delta Flight 1183."

"What do you mean, you're not getting a response?"

"Like I said, the pilot's not responding."

"Then get the hell down here so I can *see* you when I'm *talking* to you," he said, his frustration bubbling to the surface.

It was now 9:30 AM The fax crackled and several pages with names listed in long columns rolled out. Ed grabbed the pages before they could hit the drop box and uncapped a Sharpie.

As John looked over his shoulder, Ed began with the manifest for American Flight 11, circling names that jumped out at him. Arabic men had carried out the attack on the World Trade Center in 1993. Now, as the television showed smoke emanating from the World Trade Center again, this time so much bigger, so much worse, he looked for Arabic names.

In 2A and 2B, he circled two, both W. Alshehri.

In 8D, M. Atta, and 8G, A. Alomari.

In 10B, he circled S. Alsuqami.

The remainder of the plane—the other ninety-two passengers—did not appear suspicious as he glided the tip of the Sharpie down the page.

Then Ed turned to the manifest for United Flight 175, and did the same thing with his pen. He circled F. Alquadibanihammad, A. Alghamdi, H. Alghamdi, M. Alshehri, and M. Alsehhi.

"FBI here yet?" he asked John.

"They're on the way over from downtown."

"Tell 'em we got their guys."

Chapter Five
KATHRYN

T HREE DAYS before 9/11, on September 9. 2001, Kathryn Barbour, a twenty-five year veteran flight attendant with American Airlines and a personal friend of mine for nearly as long, flew from Dulles to LA with gardening on her mind.

American Airlines offered four daily nonstops from Dulles International to Los Angeles: 8:10 AM, 11 AM, 3 PM, and the 5:30 PM, but Kathryn had bid on the 3 PM flight Sunday so she could turn around the next morning. Fall was coming, and she had neglected her yard. Guilt was fast setting in. Time to mulch my beloved camellias, she chided herself.

Because of the quick nature of her trip, American put her up Sunday night at a hotel near LAX, the international airport in Los Angeles. If a layover is going to be longer than twelve hours, the airline puts the crew up in Marina del Ray, which is nice because flight attendants can rent bikes and explore the beach through Venice to Santa Monica. But this was a fast turnaround and though departing planes seemed to start their engines in the foyer, at least this wasn't that other hotel, the one with the enclosed courtyard where you had to stare up twenty stories to see daylight. This one had a view of the Pacific sky, and Kathryn endured the noise for the stars she knew were out there somewhere among the smog.

Look at the bright side, she told herself. Always look at the bright side. That was Kathyrn.

On Monday, September 10, Flight 76 departed LAX at 8:30 AM. Kathryn was thankful for the early start, since that meant she would be back at Dulles by 4:30 PM.

Nice, she thought, not too late that I won't still be fresh when I get up Tuesday morning, slip on old jeans, and venture into the backyard, her "sanctuary," with garden gloves and trowel.

———————

Kathryn had grown up in Indiana, just across the Ohio River from the Cincinnati airport. As a young girl, she would play in her backyard and watch the planes fly low above the trees on their approach to the airport. Each time a plane passed she would crane her neck and dream of far away places. Following flight attendant training in the fall of 1976, Kathryn was sent to the Washington, D.C base, where after unpacking her bags, she was assigned her first trip.

"I was attracted to the job for its self-sufficient quality," she said, noting also how she'd barely had time to fold clothes and put silverware in a drawer in her new apartment before setting out. "I had to check into a hotel I had never stayed at, then make my way back to the airport again for another flight at dawn. It was a whirl, this new, self-sufficient life, but the truth is, I loved it!"

Many flight attendants, Kathryn included, will tell you the same thing: they like the job because it demands rigorous attention to detail and commitment to a regimen during a flight, but once the plane lands and they are off-airport, heading to a hotel in a city far from home, their time is theirs.

"We're free," said Kathryn. "I can't tell you how many times I've gotten to a new place, hopped a bus, and headed out to explore the local attractions. That's what I've always wanted to do, ever since I was a young girl in my backyard watching planes. I wanted to visit new places and experience something new and surprising every day."

With 800 flight attendants and 200 pilots stationed in Washington, the "DCA base," as American Airlines calls it, was a small, close-knit operation, prompting many of the flight attendants to become friends. It was such the nature of the job, to be self-sufficient and independent, that many became as close as siblings.

"If I was on the road and got sick, my first instinct would be to call another flight attendant," Kathryn said.

But the flip side of a flight attendant's busy life had its appeal too, including days when you could get home after a quick coast to coast turnaround and anticipate a quiet morning the next day working in your garden.

As her flight from Los Angeles approached Dulles that Monday afternoon, September 10, the captain, pilot Charles Burlingame, came on the public address and asked the flight attendants to prepare the cabin for landing.

"I didn't know Chic was working this flight," said another flight attendant as she and Kathryn gathered refuse on a final pass up the aisle before strapping themselves into jump seats at the back of the plane.

"I talked to him at the gate in Los Angeles before we came on," Kathryn said. That was her practice; she always tried to meet the captain before departure. She liked Burlingame, called "Chic" by his friends. He was hard-working—a stickler for the rules—and she respected that.

"I heard it's his birthday Wednesday," said her friend. "Someone said he's planning to celebrate in LA. He'll need to turn right around. What a surprise?" The two laughed, since everyone who flew with Chic knew he was always on the go.

Chic had a discipline honed at the Naval Tactical Warfare and Strategic Air Command School in Annapolis, nicknamed "Top Gun," that was perfected while flying the Navy's F-4 Phantom jets.

And he was adamant about safety. One day on approach to LAX, controllers in the tower told him to switch his assigned runway at the last minute, but he refused and instead chose to circle around the airport. He regarded his passengers' safety as his greatest trust.

For a time Chic had flown regularly to South America, but he never felt comfortable with the approach to Bogotá airport. Shortly after he gave up the route in 1989, one of the pilots who replaced him crashed into the Columbia mountainside. Chic himself had eluded death several times. In the Navy he had often landed his Phantom jets on aircraft carrier decks as the ships had pitched in rough seas, but those dangerous experiences had shaped him. Chic knew the whimsical nature of fate, the dangers of flying and the uncertainties of the job, but that's what a pilot did. Pilots go up in the air never knowing what might happen, but each does his or her best to minimize the risks.

"Is Chic planning to go back?" asked her friend. "Did he talk about that at the gate?"

"I don't know his plans," said Kathryn.

She didn't know that he had tickets to a baseball game in LA on the evening of September 11, that he and his brother, Brad, had planned to celebrate Chic's birthday at a California Angels game, near where they had grown up in Orange Country. She didn't know that Chic's wife, Sheri, an American Airlines flight attendant, planned to go, but that Chic had told her the seats Brad had gotten weren't great and suggested that she should wait in Washington, that he'd come home after the game to celebrate with her.

"We didn't talk about plans," Kathyrn said. "We talked about time."

Well, "whatever he does, one thing we know, he won't be late," said her friend.

Again the two laughed, since Chic's uncanny ability with time was legendary. Flight attendants knew how, with his supreme efficiency, Chic could make up time in flight as well as any pilot. Often he would trim forty-five minutes off a coast-to-coast trip and bring a late departure in early.

"All I remember is he kept tapping his watch," Kathryn said. "Time to go, time to go."

Soon the plane swooped down and the wheels touched ground in Dulles, early of course, and Kathryn and her friend smiled.

After the plane reached the gate and the cabin door was opened, Kathryn waited at the rear of the plane. That was her job, to wait for all passengers to exit. Then she walked to the front of the plane, the last to leave. Kathryn poked her head in the cabin to look for Chic; she wanted to thank him for a good flight, another of her practices, but he was already gone.

Ah! she thought. Typical Chic. Never one to sit still.

Kathyrn stepped off the plane, wheeling her Travelpro bag behind her, but as she left that evening she regretted that she had not had a chance to say good-bye.

Chapter Six

TONI AND MICHELLE

AT 5 AM ON Tuesday morning, September 11, Toni Knisley sat down at her desk in the American Airlines flight services office at Reagan National Airport in Washington, DC, to begin her day.

Toni had started with American Airlines as a secretary in 1986. She had worked her way up by working hard, taking every possible job in the office, from clerical positions to operations before becoming the flight service manager, second in command to Rosemary Dillard, the flight service base manager. Toni was a tireless worker, but with a great laugh. Run something ironic by Toni, and you'd get a great laugh, with her head tossed back. "Oh, come on!" she'd say. She was famous for "oh, come on!"

Toni had grown up in the small town of Mt. Vernon, Indiana. Her mother had been poor—but smart—and became a college administrator. Toni's father, a machinist, eventually took a job with the space program, which required the family to move to San Diego. There, Toni met and married a Navy man, and they moved to Washington, DC, which is where Toni was in 1986 when the call came from American Airlines.

Because of her tireless work habits, friends and co-workers considered her the "glue" that held everything together, a depiction borne out as she worked her way up to a senior position at the station in Washington, DC. It was a reputation she had earned by being the first one into the office every morning, which is what she was again the morning of September 11, when her phone rang.

"Do you miss me?" asked the voice on the other end.

"Who is this?"

"It's me, Toni. It's Michelle!"

Michelle Heidenberger, a veteran flight attendant who had started her career with American Airlines in 1971, flew regular "turns" out of Reagan to Dallas. Michelle was a tall, dark-haired woman with a quick smile. She was married to a pilot with US Airways, Tommie Heidenberger, and they had two kids, a daughter in college and a son starting high school that fall. Michelle loved to tease Toni, to see if she could elicit an "oh, come on!" The two had a lot in common— they were the same age, both had two kids—and they loved to talk about the challenges and delights of raising a family. Still, it caught Toni off guard to be getting a call from Michelle, rather than seeing her in the doorway at Reagan.

"Michelle! Where are you?"

"I'm at Dulles."

"Oh, come on! What are you doing at Dulles? Aren't you flying your regular turn to Dallas today?"

"I'm working Flight 77 to L.A. because I want to take time off in October to go to Italy with Tommie and the kids. I've been bidding Dulles, to build up time. Be sure you tell Rosemary how hard I'm working." Rosemary Dillard, the flight service manager, was Toni's boss. When Toni talked, Rosemary listened.

"I will. Listen you get back here soon, you hear . . . Michelle?" Toni could hear voices behind Michelle, voices telling her it was time to go, the voices of the other flight attendants she'd be working with that day.

"Listen, Toni, I gotta go. Chic and David are on the plane already. Ken and Jennifer, Renee, they need me on the plane, too."

"You get back here, you hear."

"Remember to tell Rosemary how hard I'm working. Tell her to give me some good turns on the bid sheet."

"I will, but you come see me when you're at Reagan next."

"Always," she said.

Then she was gone.

Much about Flight 77—the flight back to L.A. that Kathryn Barbour had come in on the evening before—remains a mystery, even today.

After departing from Dulles at 8:20 AM, the plane flew west over Virginia and West Virginia without incident until 8:46. Then suddenly it turned north. Several minutes later, the plane turned around and flew south again. During this period the plane traveled off course by about fifteen miles and remained off course for five minutes. At 8:56 AM, flight controllers tried to make contact with the pilot once they saw that the transponder, the device that sends and receives the exact location of a plane in flight, had been turned off. According to regulations, a military fighter jet should have been sent up to see what was going on. There are very strict rules on this. If a pilot in flight does not answer a call from an FAA tower, then fighter jets are required to be dispatched to find out why. But this time, no plane was sent up by NORAD (North American Aerospace Defense Command) to look for Flight 77. The lapse remains unexplained.

While this was occurring, American Airlines Flight 11 out of Boston struck the World Trade Center's North Tower, as a second plane, United 175, with Marianne and Jesus aboard, flew south from Boston toward New York. Across the Hudson at Newark Airport, United Airlines Flight 93 lifted off after a long delay on the taxiway and ascended toward its cruising altitude.

With its transponder off, Flight 77 flew east toward Washington at four hundred miles per hour. FAA flight controllers continued to try to make contact with the cockpit in the minutes following 9 AM, but without success.

On Flight 77, flight attendant Renee May called her father in an attempt to reach Toni Knisley, while a passenger, Barbara Olsen, a television commentator, called her husband, United States Solicitor General Ted Olsen. Barbara told him she was standing in a bathroom at the back of the plane. She asked Ted what she should do. This occurred at 9:25, nearly half an hour after Flight 77 had turned around and headed back east.

Barbara Olsen's call cut out, but five minutes later she called her husband back, telling him that all the passengers had been herded to the rear of the plane. Hijackers had used knives and box cutters to overtake the plane, she said. Her husband asked her to describe what she saw out the window, and she told him she just saw houses. "What should I do?" she asked.

At 9:33, radar showed the plane crossing the Capitol Beltway, on a path toward the Pentagon. It continued past the Pentagon at an altitude of seven thousand feet before making a high-speed arc in the vicinity of the White House. Then, in the air over the city, it angled back around and turned toward the Pentagon once again.

At 9:37, the blip radar technicians had been watching disappeared from their screens, just as a fireman, Alan Wallace, heard a loud roar on the path from the parking lot to the Pentagon. He looked up to see a huge jet twenty-five feet off the ground headed directly toward him. Alan dove under a car as the plane passed over his head, its engines screaming.

At 9:38, Flight 77 tore into the west side of the Pentagon.

Chapter Seven
SUE

ALL AIRPORTS have a plan for emergencies. It's an FAA requirement that each United States airport perform a "table top," a session where key players involved with the emergency plan sit around a table and go through a mock drill once a year. In addition, all airports are required to go through a full-scale dress rehearsal every three years.

Under Sue Baer's direction, Newark conducts a full-scale emergency dress rehearsal every year. Airport emergency plans focus on aircraft emergencies. In the old *Airport Certification Manual* (current at the time, but revised after 9/11), the emergency drill was called "Chapter 17." Specifically, the section breaks out the details for emergency response in cases such as:

- Aircraft incidents and accidents
- Bomb incidents, including a designated parking area for aircraft suspected of having a bomb on board
- Structural fires
- Natural disasters
- Crowd control and measures to prevent unlawful interference with operations
- Radiological incidents
- Medical services
- Removal of disabled aircraft

"But no place in the manual does it tell you what do for a day like September 11," said Sue. And so she responded instinctively.

"Once I realized we were under attack, I made it clear to the tower, no more planes going out," she said. "Until we know where these planes are coming from, that's it, no more departures. Newark airport is closed."

New York's two other major airports—JFK and LaGuardia—followed her lead and shut down also at her suggestion. At 9:17, FAA headquarters in Washington, D.C, gave an official order to close the three New York airports.

Sue's action at 9:03—and the complementary response by her fellow Port Authority managers at JFK and LaGuardia to close—may have saved lives. No one knows for sure whether any planes sitting with their engines running on the tarmac at New York's three airports between 9:03—when Sue gave her order—and 9:17, when the FAA acted, carried potential hijackers. But the fact remains that in those fourteen minutes, with a plane taking off every thirty seconds, seventy-five planes at Newark, Kennedy, and LaGuardia had their departures aborted as a result of Sue's command.

Seventy-five additional planes that would have been in the air out of New York City that morning never got off the ground.

Working from "Chapter 17," Sue deployed available resources identified in the plan, improvising as she went along.

"It was surreal," she said later. "I stood in the operations office on the fourth floor in Building 10 with my team, looking out over the flats to our home, the World Trade Center, being attacked. The towers were burning and getting worse, and I kept thinking: 'how many people do I know in there right now? Hundreds! Hundreds upon hundreds! Twenty-six years I had worked for the Port Authority, fourteen of them in the World Trade Center, and now I had to stare across the meadowlands at that terrible sight.

"I thought of so many friends and colleagues. Everyone in the Port Authority knows everyone. This one married that one. The cousin of another married yet another. We're a family, and yet I couldn't think of that, I had a job to do—we all had a job to do.

"In order, these were my concerns: first, secure the airside—the area from the terminals to the perimeter gates, including the runways. This is done by securing all terminal gates and doors that lead to the airside, as well as securing perimeter gates that provide access to the airside. Next, get people out of the terminals. Third, I wanted to provide information, though it was not forthcoming to us. I had very little to go on, but I still wanted to pass on what we knew, while we tried to comfort people."

On top of all this, Sue worried what might happen next. "Thoughts kept racing through my mind. Are we, meaning the Port Authority, under attack? Newark is a Port Authority facility. Was that their plan, whoever was doing this? Were they going to start crashing planes into us next?

"My thought was that I've got thousands of people at this airport at the moment. I had to protect them. And so I gathered my team to deal with it all."

Sue had good people. John Jacoby, manager of airport services, had been with her the longest. They had shared offices next to each other in the World Trade Center beginning in the early nineties. John did not have an academic background in aviation operations, but he had "the smarts," as Sue said of his talents, including two Masters degrees. Twice he had spent time in the Peace Corps, both times in Nepal.

"The Peace Corps taught me how to separate out the important things in life," John said. "Often, I would meet mothers who lived in rural areas of the mountains who had difficult choices to make. For example: do I walk two days and cross three mountain peaks to take my sick child to a village on the chance a doctor may be there, or do I stay in my hut and hope the baby improves because I don't want to leave my other children unattended during a snow storm?"

Sue liked John for the intelligence and common sense he brought to the job. "Life is a balance, and we're constantly called upon to make hard choices," she said. "Nobody makes better choices than John Jacoby."

Assessing the situation, Sue instructed her staff to call the airport contractors. Newark was in the middle of an ambitious redevelopment plan and, as such, the contractors controlled heavy equipment, bulldozers and the like, which could be pressed into action.

She asked the contractors to load up barriers and place them in front of the access gates to seal off the aeronautical area. An aviation facilities department, which includes the maintenance department, is responsible for making sure that all the equipment at an airport is in good working condition. Since the aviation department leases out terminal gates (and other space in the terminal) to the airlines, concessions, and others, those entities have their own maintenance operations to handle their equipment. Hence, the facilities department focuses on the facility itself, meaning its primary attention is on the runways, taxiways, terminal infrastructure, curbside, and roadways leading into the airport, along with such things as the heating and cooling systems and plumbing.

"We didn't know if whoever was doing this might storm the airport next," Sue continued. "Were they going to crash their way onto the runways? We were flying in the dark, nobody could tell us anything, and so we acted as best we could according to our emergency plan."

All the while, rumors—mostly coming from TV—swirled. Some reports said hundreds had been killed already at the World Trade Center. Other reports said the number was in the thousands. New York City Mayor Rudy Giuliani, when asked by a reporter for his estimate of the losses, said, "It is going to be greater than any of us can comprehend."

Sue's director of facilities, Trevor Liddle, still had not heard from his wife, Laurie. She had been on the 83rd floor in Tower One when the first plane had stuck at 8:46 AM. The plane had hit several floors above her—on the 90th floor—and she told Trevor she was going to try to get out. But time passed and still he had not heard. All his life he had tried to keep a stiff upper lip. It's what had gotten him through tough times before, but how do you deal with something like this?

When Sue saw him, she asked, "Any word from Laurie yet?"

He shook his head, and Sue gave him a hug. It was the first of many she would offer that morning.

"After we fortified the airside, next we focused on evacuating people," said Sue, recalling that terrible day. "Once the FAA issued a national ground stop at 9:26, it was clear we weren't going to be reopening the airport any time soon. We had to take care of the people on site."

That was easier said than done. In 2001, Newark served 34 million travelers a year. Each day, 1450 flights operated in and out of the facility. At 9 AM on that morning, fifty-thousand people filled the airport concourses, seeking either to come or go. By 9:30, groups of departing passengers were heading out of the terminals as others, unaware of the magnitude of the events, continued their march toward the gate areas. There, they mixed with people arriving from planes that were returning as a result of Sue's order to close the airport, and passengers from planes that were arriving as part of regular scheduled service.

It made for a volatile mix.

"Our goal became clear after 9:26 and the FAA ground stop," said Sue. "We had to get fifty-thousand people to a location that was not Newark airport."

She called her staff to move down to the third floor, into the major conference room where they could set up a war room to plan and execute from the improvised plan they were creating from "Chapter 17."

In the windowless conference room, a television sat in a wooden cabinet behind two loose-hinged doors. The TV worked, but since they couldn't get cable, the picture was fuzzy. As Sue and her team spread papers across the conference table, someone turned on the TV. For a moment, the room went silent as the picture—fuzzy as it was—showed the twin columns of smoke emanating from the World Trade Center.

No one said a word.

The only sound was the television commentator repeating what everyone knew, that two planes had struck the North and South Towers of the World Trade Center in New York City and the number of casualties was yet to be determined.

"Call Captain Kormash; see if they've called the cities of Newark and Elizabeth," Sue said, turning away from the TV. Nick Kormash was the Port Authority chief of police at Newark. "Make sure we're getting police to the airport entrances to control traffic."

John Jacoby said he would go over to the terminals to monitor events. He wanted to see how the evacuation plan was working, and determine what additional resources might be needed.

Sue also gave orders to call the Red Cross. "Help them get set up, give them whatever they need."

Next: call the bus contractor. "Get busses mobilized and directed to the curb to start moving people out of the terminals to Penn Station Newark where they can catch trains and keep moving." The train station in Newark was still functioning, they learned after a call was made.

More orders: check hotels. "We're going to have people with no place to go. How many rooms are available?"

Another order: call concessions, tell them to stay open. "People need food," she said. "And what about baby formula, and diapers? Make sure there's an adequate supply in the emergency closet. We're going to need them."

And Gateway Security. "Call Gateway. Make sure all available customer service reps are dispatched to the terminals. We need staff to move passengers to the curbs so the busses, taxis, whatever vehicles we can enlist, can move them out."

Suddenly, Sue heard her name being called from the doorway. It was her secretary, who wore a worried expression.

"What?"

"Captain Kormash on the phone for you."

Nick Kormash knew his role: secure all airport entrances and exits. He and Sue had talked briefly in the minutes after 9 AM, but now he was calling back. Not a good sign.

Sue hurried to her office across from the conference room. "Nick?" she asked.

"A plane just hit the Pentagon."

It was 9:42, three minutes after American Airlines Flight 77 had crashed into the Pentagon in Washington, DC.

"Any more out there?"

"Don't know."

Sue hung up with Nick and returned to the conference room. By the time she walked back through the door, everyone was staring at the fuzzy TV. The dateline said: Washington, DC. The outline of the building on fire, the Pentagon, was unmistakable.

Sue took a deep breath. In the doorway, her secretary appeared again, "Channel 4 on the phone."

"I can't talk to them."

"They want to know if the airport is safe."

"We'll do a press conference later."

"What time?"

"Two o'clock. Building 80. I can't talk to them right now."

She turned to read Trevor Liddle's face, for any new sign about Laurie. He maintained his stiff upper lip, staying strong while he continued to speak on the phone with contractors, coordinating the Jersey barriers.

Across the conference table, Frank Loprano spoke on his cell phone. Cell phone coverage had become spotty, but his still worked while he spoke with one of his supervisors. Nearly fifty planes had been redirected back to their gates after Sue's order to close the airport, and people were coming off their aircraft and returning to the terminals with two questions: "What's happening?" And, "What's going to happen next?"

Frank had been trained as an engineer, and he maintained his measured, analytical approach. "Keep the passengers in the terminals calm," he said. Then, suddenly, he was passed a note from one of the office staff. The note said that his secretary, Anne Leahy, had not been heard from that morning.

He put his supervisor on hold and called to an office outside for more details. "Where is she?" he asked.

"She had a training seminar in the World Trade Center."

"Any one talk to her?"

"Last night she said she was going to drive into Jersey City and catch the first bus to the World Trade Center. That's all we know."

Frank took a deep breath as he gave directions to his duty managers to keep everyone getting off the planes calm. "Move them smoothly, without panic, to the curb where people in landside can arrange busses for them."

Sue saw Frank stretch to maintain his measured tone.

"Anne?" she asked, and he nodded.

"Where is she?"

"She went to the World Trade Center this morning for a training class."

Sue gave him a hug as her secretary once again appeared in the doorway. "Yes?" Sue asked.

"Al Graser at JFK. He needs you to call him back. It's important." Al, the general manager at JFK, had been on the phone with Sue at 9:03. He had closed his airport at her urging. Now he was calling back.

Again, she rushed to her office, where Ernie, "the phone guy," pulled on some wires, and pushed on others. Ernie was a spark-plug of a man in a Verizon uniform.

"Central system is out," Ernie said. "Fire in the World Trade's knocked the crap outta the whole damn system."

"Can you get me a line?"

"The one on your desk still works."

"Thanks, Ernie," she said, as she picked up her phone and dialed JFK.

"Al?"

"You've got one, Sue," said Al, who picked up on the first ring.

"What do you mean?"

"United Flight 93. It was scheduled to leave Newark at 8 AM."

"What about it?"

"It's missing."

"Jesus!"

"It got off the ground at 8:40. That's all I know. That's all my sources could tell me."

Again, she returned to the conference room.

"We've got Gateway security agents in all the terminals," said John Jacoby, returning from his sortie into the field. "They're keeping everyone calm. We had some people out on the roadways, trying to walk out of the airport, but we got a couple trucks going around now to pick them up."

People read Sue's face. They waited for her to speak. "United Flight 93 is missing," she said.

"From Newark?"

"It was scheduled to depart at 8 AM. It departed at 8:40."

"Where is it?"

She pointed to the window. "Out there, somewhere. I don't know. But we've got to plan in the event it may be heading back here."

"Is it?"

"I don't know. But we've got to prepare as if it is." A long moment passed.

"We've got another problem," said Huntley Lawrence, supervisor of landside operations, who took a call on his cell phone.

"What?" cried Sue. "What now?"

"The police aren't letting anyone into the airport. They've got a huge crowd at the main entrance. Police from Newark and Elizabeth are turning everybody away. It's a zoo out there."

"No, no, no," said Sue. "We've got to let people *in* if we're going to get people *out!* Send someone out to the airport entrances. Tell them to work with the police to use judgment. If it's an aunt or an uncle or brother or sister—someone coming here to pick somebody up—let them in! Get me a phone. Let me talk to the Port Authority police . . ."

But as Sue spoke, the room went silent. She turned in the direction of all the heads as people turned to the fuzzy TV.

"Oh, my God!" Sue's stomach sank as if tethered to a stone. "Oh, no!" she said. The room remained silent, all but for the whoosh, the awful, horrible sinking sound of the South Tower, World Trade Two. They all stood stock still as the tower crumbled in on itself and ten seconds later fell to the ground.

It was 10 AM.

Three minutes later, Flight 93, which had departed Newark forty minutes late after being delayed on the tarmac, crashed into a field in Shanksville, Pennsylvania. Within minutes, smoke could be seen rising out of a farmer's field on the fuzzy TV as the picture switched back and forth from the smoldering wreckage of the South Tower to the fire at the Pentagon in Washington, DC, to the field under a blue sky in western Pennsylvania.

Sue turned to John Jacoby. "Where does it end?" They had been together the longest, and had experienced the first attack together in 1993.

He shook his head.

At that moment, Sal D'Orio passed in the hallway. Their eyes met, Sue's and his. Sue didn't say anything. She knew Sal, who headed up structural maintenance, had a son who worked in the World Trade Center.

"Sal?" she asked.

He smiled, a wan one, but a smile nevertheless. "He's okay," he said. "I just got a call. He got out."

"Thank God," she said, and she hugged him.

Chapter Eight

TONI, ROSEMARY, DEBBIE, AND KATHRYN

A<small>FTER HANGING</small> up with her friend Michelle, Toni Knisley went back to work in the American Airlines flight service office at Reagan National when shortly before 9 AM, her phone rang. Jimmy Baker from maintenance was on the line from one of the hangers.

"Toni, have you heard about something happening?"

"Happening? What do you mean?"

"I just got a call from my parents. They said a missile hit the World Trade Center."

"Missile? What do you mean a missile?"

"Check it out and call me, will you? We don't have any TVs over here."

"Sure," she said, and she walked across the hall to the crew lounge where several people were watching TV, eyes wide. Reports told of a small plane that had hit the World Trade Center. Suddenly the half dozen or so people in the room gasped as the shot showed the explosion of a second plane hitting the South Tower. Toni turned and hurried back to her office to call Jimmy, but his line was busy. In seconds, all the phones in the office began ringing. Toni ran to answer them, but a secretary interrupted her.

"Toni, I just got a strange call. Renee May's father is on the line."

"Renee's father?" asked Toni.

"Yes, he just got a call from Renee, who was calling from her plane. She tried to get through to the office, to talk to you, but all the lines were busy, so she called her parents. She told her father her plane was hijacked."

"What!"

"Renee said everyone had been pushed to the back of the plane by the hijackers. She told her father to call us, to tell us what's going on."

"Where's her father now?" asked Toni.

"I put him on hold."

"Ask him to wait. I'll check it out."

Toni rushed to her office, where she sat down at the computer. She knew Renee's employee number. These were her people, and she knew all her flight attendants by heart. She punched in Renee's number to call up her schedule. There it was. Flight 77, Dulles to Los Angeles, scheduled to depart at 8:10.

My God, she thought! That was Michelle's flight, too!

She tried to log onto the flight to view its status, but information was blocked. Was the plane still flying? Where was it? She looked at her watch. It was 9:28.

Toni called her boss, Rosemary Dillard, who was upstairs attending a weekly senior staff meeting. Moments later, Rosemary rushed through Toni's door.

"Rosemary, something's happening."

"I know."

"Two planes hit the World Trade Center."

"I know, we saw the replay on TV in the Admiral's Club."

"We got a call from Renee May's father. I'm afraid she might have been on that plane, the second one that hit the World Trade Center."

"What?" Rosemary exclaimed.

"Renee called her parents and said her plane had been hijacked. I think that might have been her plane, Renee's, the one that hit the second tower."

"Oh, no!"

"I tried to call up the flight on the computer, but I couldn't get it."

"What flight is it?"

"Flight 77 out of Dulles. Michelle was on it too," said Toni.

"No, that can't be!"

"I called it up on Renee's schedule. That's her flight. I'm sure of it."

"No!" Rosemary said, as she stumbled backward, her hands cupping her mouth, she collapsed into a chair.

"Rosemary! What's the matter?"

"No," she said, shaking her head. "No!"

"What's the matter?"

"I put my husband Eddie on that flight this morning!"

———————

Debbie Roland, Kathryn Barbour's basemate in Washington, DC, became a flight attendant after experiencing air travel at any early age, and later found that transportation was in her genes. Her grandfather had been a railroad man, and her father's career was space, starting with the Titan Missile Program, so it was not a stretch for Debbie to take her first job, at age sixteen, at a local travel agency. Debbie took the job knowing that as soon as she got out of school, she would apply to the airlines.

Airline safety was not a sophisticated system in the 1970s. In those days the focus after an accident was on the cause of a crash. It was only with time, as data became more available, that the focus shifted to "survivability," including looking at ways to mitigate the effects of air turbulence, in-flight fires, and other accidental occurrences.

Debbie became a leader in the safety effort at American. She became a union official with APFA (Association of Professional Flight Attendants), one of five attendant unions, and worked on committees that explored intervention strategies to reduce injuries and save lives in the event of air accidents.

She now flew out of the Washington, DC, base. The night before September 11, she had tried to fax a document to the National

Transportation Safety Bureau (NTSB). For some reason the fax wasn't going through. So she decided to take the train into town early on Tuesday and stop at the NTSB to deliver the document personally.

While Debbie was standing in the NTSB lobby Tuesday morning waiting for someone to come down and accept the document, her cell phone rang. It was shortly before 9 AM. Her union colleague, Kathy Lord Jones, APFA's national safety coordinator, was calling from Dallas.

"Where are you?" Kathy asked.

"I'm at NTSB. What's up?"

"One of our planes has been involved in a hijacking. Leave your cell phone on. Gotta go."

Debbie hung up. She looked through the glass partition at a dozen TVs in the NTSB control room. Most were tuned to news programs, local and cable, when one by one the words, SPECIAL BULLETIN, appeared on the screen. She could see, but she could not hear through the thick glass. Still, she knew something was up as the images on the TV switched to New York and shots of the World Trade Center. Just then, the door opened and a man appeared. He stared over her shoulder, looking distracted.

"What's going on?" she asked.

"A small plane hit the World Trade Center."

"A small plane?"

"That's the report," he said, and he ducked back inside, closing the door, sealing her off from the sound. Debbie pressed up against the broad expanse of glass, feeling it cool against her nose, but her heart was racing. Small plane? What about our plane? Where is our plane?

It was then that she watched the second plane hit, and it was the equivalent of a solid blow to her stomach. "Oh, my God!

The doors opened and several NTSB officials rushed into the control room. Debbie tried to intercept them, but they shook her off and gathered in tight knots in front of the televisions. She stood watching, not aware of time, not aware of anything except the second shock to her stomach. Eventually she heard her name called.

"Miss Roland?"

It was the NTSB official she had been waiting for, the person she had called to come to the lobby to pick up the document.

"Do you want to come downstairs . . . to my office?" he asked. "Will that be more comfortable?"

"Yes," she said, "downstairs."

More comfortable was a relative term, under the circumstances. The blow she had absorbed to her stomach had not subsided, yet she summoned all her strength and energy to do as she had been trained to do, to think clearly.

At that moment, a second accident investigator approached Debbie.

"It's your plane," he said grimly.

"Our plane?"

"An American Airlines flight out of Boston," he said.

Debbie called Kathy Lord Jones, and Kathy verified the awful truth, that the initial reports had been mistaken. It had not been a small plane that had crashed into the World Trade Center, but instead it had been "their" plane, an American Airlines flight that had departed from Boston's Logan airport.

As she stood in the cramped NTSB office, watching the image of the World Trade Center burning, Debbie looked at the hole in the building and the smoke, and she thought, *those are our people.* She wanted to help, she was a safety expert, but what could she do?

"Do you have any new details?" she asked Kathy, who was somber as she read off the names of the crew on AAL Flight 11 and then the names of the crew on Flight 77. This was the first confirmation that AAL flight 77 and her Washington colleagues had crashed into the Pentagon.

Her plane. Her airport. Her colleagues.

What Debbie recalled, and would always remember, was the way Kathy had recited the names, calling each of the pilots and flight attendants by their first names, Chic, David, Michelle, Renee, Ken, and Jennifer.

But that was natural, Debbie realized in that awful moment, because that's how she knew them too, by their first names. They were her colleagues.

The first thing Kathryn did upon waking that bright, blue morning after returning home from L.A. the evening before was make a cup of tea. It was so nice to be home, she thought as she brewed the tea in her kitchen and looked out the high arched window to her lush garden. When your work involves going fast enough—and high enough—to cover a mile every seven seconds, it's nice to look out the window and see the garden—her connection to the rejuvenating power of life—sitting still.

Kathryn stepped outside and took a deep breath. Aromatic air filled her lungs, and she thought: the swing! Enough of speed, she wanted to feel the softened pace, slow things way down, so she sat on her swing below the big maple on a bluff at the back of her yard. She was sitting, swinging gently back and forth, when her husband, opened a back door.

"Kathryn," he said. "I just heard a report that a plane hit the World Trade Center in New York."

"A plane?"

"A small plane, they say."

Her first thought as she stopped swinging was, "That's strange. It's so nice here in DC. But it must be foggy in New York." She hopped off the swing and hurried into the house, quickening her pace.

Inside the house, she stood, mouth agape, as she watched the picture on the television, the black smoke rising like a spreading stain against the sky.

At some point, after a second plane struck, and she stood with her hands cupped over her mouth, the TV cut to the Pentagon and another fire.

"Speculation is that it could be another plane," said the announcer.

Kathryn continued to stare, listening to the speculation, before she decided to go to the computer. The computer might have updates more quickly, she thought, and on the computer she might get hard news, something to cut through the endless stream of rumors coming from the television.

She took a deep breath, part of her training to stay calm, as she worked the keys, trying to get information, something, anything, when she heard the words on the TV behind her. The words were stark and bold and took her breath away.

"We have a report that the plane that stuck the Pentagon is American Airlines Flight 77," said the announcer.

She stood, her breath gone, as the picture focused on the fire at the Pentagon. She had worked Flight 77 hundreds of times.

Oh, my God, who's working today, she thought.

Again she cupped her mouth, but she did not cry out, because that is what she had been trained to do, to stay calm.

Chapter Nine
MARK AND STEVE

Wᴴᴱɴ ᴍᴀʀᴋ ʜᴜssᴇʏ, United Airline's station manager at Logan, was a boy growing up in Roslindale, Massachusetts, a Boston working class neighborhood, he had no idea what he wanted to do with his life. Then one night he encountered a pilot at a career fair at Catholic Memorial, his high school, and all that changed. Tall like a basketball player, but more introspective than interested in athletics, Hussey hung on every word as a pilot boasted about how flying made it "easy to get around," and "pilots made a lot of money." In the car on the way home Hussey told his dad that he had found the thing he wanted to be when he grew up.

"Son, you've just been introduced to the first great sales pitch in your life," his dad said, but Hussey remained resolute—he was going to work in aviation.

After a year of college in Nova Scotia and a stint in the Air Force in Alaska, Mark was living in Maine with his wife and two young children. He was driving a Coke truck part-time, when his wife brought home a copy of the *Bangor Daily News*. Together they got out a magic marker and went through the want ads with the red marker circling anything that looked promising. They came up with three candidates for permanent employment for him: a regular job with Coke, a job at the front desk at a local motel and a job with United Airlines.

His son, age six, wanted him to take the job with Coke for the hats, tee-shirts, and free six packs, but Mark knew life was about to open for him.

He took the job with United.

Mark first worked at United's small station in Bangor, where as a ramp agent, he got to sell tickets, check baggage, and—from his Air Force days this appealed to him—watch the mechanics work. His search had begun at a pilot's booth in his high school gym, but now he had found his passion: aviation operations. He liked problems, a chance to analyze causes and suggest solutions. Before long senior staff at United noticed too: in this tall, beanpole of a guy with the easy, likeable manner they had a troubleshooting phenom, and up the ladder he went.

Mark was working to systemize United's customer service in Boston when I met him in 2001. He had researched the "chain" of customer contacts, from the moment a customer stepped inside the terminal to the time the plane lifted off. He had identified the customer "contacts" from the cabin, to maintenance, to on-board, ramp, customer service reps, and operations and created focus groups to let his employees tell him what they believed was required to enhance the experience for the customer. In essence, he told his people, "United plans to spend 100 million dollars to expand our operation in Boston. If we don't work as a team, then we will be like any dysfunctional family. We will waste 100 million dollars and your jobs will disappear."

He conducted an exhaustive search for the right person to manage his customer service department and hired Steve Bolognese, a former USAir manager, who brought me on board in the spring of 2001. I clearly remember meeting Mark. The tall beanpole part stuck me immediately, along with how quickly he got to the point. "Got any customer service ideas?" he had asked two seconds after shaking hands.

I told him about an airport director I had worked with at Oakland who had allowed his staff to order a dunk tank to celebrate an achievement at the station. The staff set the dunk tank up in the administrative area behind the ticket counter and agents took turns going around back to toss balls at a target, which once they hit the bulls-eye sent the manager, Rene Perez, toppling into the cold water below.

"What airline was that?" Mark asked.

"Southwest," I said. "They do things like that."

"So do we now," he said, and he turned to Bolognese. "Steve, get your bathing suit."

"Me!" said Steve.

The night before 9/11, Mark traveled to Newark, for a meeting with his Station Manager counterparts from the eastern region. This was something the managers did regularly, and as the senior agent at Logan, Mark represented Boston.

The group was gathered in the first class lounge in United's Red Carpet Club, when Terri Rizzuto, the Newark station manager hosting the meeting, got called away to a take a call from a senior United official in her office across the concourse. A regional vice president told her that a plane had struck the World Trade.

"We think it's an American Airlines plane," he said.

Terri called her counterpart at American Airlines at Newark to offer support, if needed. Then she returned to her colleagues in the club to share the news. By then a second plane had hit the South Tower and the group went outside for a view of lower Manhattan. Soon they returned to the club, where they could watch the television, when Terry got another call.

"Mark, it's for you," she said.

"Who?"

"Boston," she said, swallowing.

Mark's face went ashen as he held the phone.

In Chicago that morning, Steve Bolognese sat in a conference room eating a continental breakfast with other customer service managers from the United system. His colleagues probed, seeking advance information about his customer service presentation, but he told them they would have to wait a few more minutes to hear details of the work he and Mark Hussey had been doing in Boston. Then someone turned on a TV at the far end of the room and said, "Hey, something's happening."

Steve, a spirited Italian-American, is a self-starter, full of energy. He's always been that way, his colleagues will tell you, eager, constantly looking for action—always the first to pop up out of his seat, which he did now.

As a kid growing up in Ipswich, Massachusetts, Steve had traveled past Logan airport regularly with his younger sister to visit their father in East Boston. He and his sister took the trip each weekend after their parents split up, but he couldn't get enough of the planes as he passed along the airport's perimeter road. One day his dad took him to the airport entrance and said, "Let's go."

"What do you mean, let's go?"

"We're going to take a trip on an airplane."

"Airplane! You can't just get on a plane, dad."

"Sure you can," said his father.

Every year in the springtime, the Jimmie Fund, a charitable organization, offered twenty-minute airplane trips around the city of Boston on an Eastern Airline plane. That day, Steve got his first plane trip. It took his breath away. From then on, until he was a teenager, he took a Jimmie Fund flight around Boston every year and dreamed of the career he was going to have in aviation. He began that career with Piedmont Airlines as a customer service rep at JFK in New York, where just as the Jimmie Fund flight had shaped him, he was to be defined yet again by a dramatic experience.

One night a man approached him at the Piedmont counter for a flight to Richmond, Virginia. The flight had closed, and Steve was wrapping things up as the man snapped, "Get me on this flight!"

Steve had not been on the job long, but he knew how to deal with customers who barked at you: you looked up and smiled with all your teeth showing.

"I'm sorry, we closed this flight," he said.

"I need to get on this plane!" the man shouted.

"I'm sorry," Steve repeated, in the same flat tone. "The flight is closed."

"I need to be on this plane. Tonight!" the man shouted again.

"There will be another one in the morning. I'm sorry."

Then Steve did what a million customer service reps who've been insulted have done before him, he turned his back and attended to paperwork.

Five minutes later, as he completed his checklist, he looked over and saw the man sitting in a chair. The man was crying uncontrollably. Steve was new, but he knew this wasn't right. He waited a moment, then he walked over and approached the man tentatively.

"Sir, are you okay?"

The man told him his story. He had been in France on business that morning when he had received a call that his son had been killed in a car crash. Needing to get home to Richmond, he had bought a ticket on the Concorde. He had paid $3000 or whatever the fare was for the ticket, so he could get to JFK in time to catch the last Piedmont flight to Richmond that night.

"After that I learned never to presume," Steve has said often, part of the presentation on service he was prepared to give his colleagues in Chicago. "I felt terrible. As I stood in front of that man from Richmond, knowing that the flight had closed but that a greater effort on my part could have gotten him on the plane, I decided I would never again let a customer's mood determine my response. Always I would think of need from the other person's point of view, because we can never know what people have been through before they get to us."

That morning in Chicago, Steve never got to speak to his colleagues about service, as people in the room abandoned their continental breakfasts and rushed to the TV in the corner of the room.

"Steve, look!" said the fellow beside him.

The fellow was Mike Spagnuolo, United's Customer Service Manager at JFK, Steve's New York counterpart.

"Was that a second plane?" Steve asked, as a tight knot of United managers jammed around the television watching a second object strike the World Trade Center.

"Wait," said Mike. "They're going to show it again."

Steve saw it this time clearly. He swallowed hard. The reporter on the TV had been talking about "a small plane" as the source of the smoke in the first tower, but this second one, this glimmer of a shape that angled across the screen and tore into the South Tower was no small plane. Everyone could see that. It appeared silver, but on a second viewing, and then a third, Steve could make out the blue and gray of the fuselage and the familiar striping. He turned to Mike, who was already staring at him.

"Ours," Steve said.

"It's a wide-body," said Mike, "A 767."

Until that point everyone had thought the plane that had hit the North Tower was out of New York. That seemed obvious, but rumors began spreading quickly. What was happening? Who was doing this? Time stood still, even as Steve's mind raced. He couldn't tell—was it a minute, two minutes, five?—when a colleague who worked in World Headquarters walked up and stood beside him.

"They've locked down 175," he said, meaning that Flight 175 had been closed to all access in the computer system. Not a good thing!

It took a moment, as time continued to stand still, but suddenly Steve realized Flight 175 was a Boston flight, a morning non-stop to L.A.

"Oh, my God!" he thought, as he looked at Mike.

"Your plane?" said Mike.

"Oh, my God!" said Steve.

Chapter Ten
TERRI

Terri rizzuto, the United station manager at Newark, worried about Mark Hussey. She saw his face fall when he received the news from Boston about Flight 175, and understood when he said, "I've got to get out of here."

Mark scrambled to gather his possessions. He grabbed things aimlessly, stuffing items into his briefcase, as he repeated, "I've got to out of here. How do I get out of here?"

"The airport's closed," Terri said in a tone meant to soothe him. She was a lithe, five-foot, dark-haired woman, a bundle of energy, a leader, a comforter of people. At this moment she was focused completely on Mark. "Port Authority closed the airport."

"I've got to get back to Boston," he said, as he stared directly into her brown eyes.

"A car," she said. "Let's get you a car." She turned to her secretary, who read her boss' mind and made the call, calling downstairs to the ramp area to see who had a car, a van, something that could take Mark Hussey back to Boston.

"We've got to get Mark going," Terri said to the open air, then more softly, "Mark, are you okay? You going to be okay?"

He nodded as she took his hand.

Terri Rizzuto grew up in Elmont, New York, the Long Island

equivalent of Mark's working class neighborhood in Boston. It was the kind of place where a girl climbed trees and skinned knees along with the boys and never thought twice. It was the kind of neighborhood, and the kind of times—back in the mid sixties—where her mom could open the door in the morning and call again from the stoop in the evening and Terri would come running, having put in a full day playing. The experience shaped her. That's how she ran her station, skinning her knees playing with the boys, and never thinking twice.

But now all she thought about was getting Mark going, getting him back to the people who needed him. She located a van and went downstairs with him. She wanted to make sure the driver knew where to go: with traffic a mess in the city, he would need to swing north.

Mark nodded. "We'll figure it out," he said. "I've got to get going."

Terri held the door an extra second before closing it. "I'm sorry, Mark," she said, barely audible.

He squeezed her hand. "Call Steve Bolognese in Chicago," he said. "Tell him I'm on my way back to the base."

Then he was off, in a squeal of tires and dust. Terri lingered a moment to watch Mark go. She looked back in the direction of the World Trade Center. She couldn't see it for the concourse, which towered above her, but she saw the smoke rising into the sky.

"God help us!" she shuddered. She was a religious person, a deeply religious person. "God help us."

Moments later, as she stood in the concourse, the long glass corridor outside her office leading to Gates 10 to 17, she felt the gathering enormity: bridges and tunnels were closing. Airports around the country were closing. The national airspace was being shut down. "We don't know what this is all about," she said to her people as she turned and walked into her office. "But tell people for their own safety, stay calm. Don't panic. We are working to learn more."

Then her beeper buzzed shortly. It was shortly before 9:30. It was her operations station calling.

"Terri, we've got a problem."

"What problem?"

"Flight 93 is missing."

"Missing?" She repeated the word out of reflex. Terri had been in aviation ten years—as a ramp service supervisor, an in-flight supervisor, a customer service manager, and now a station manager. When she began on the ramp her boss had initially refused to hire her, calling her "too petite." Finally he did hire her, provisionally, until he made her permanent three weeks later. She was tough, he realized. She was tough. She knew what "missing" meant, the enormity of it. She swallowed hard.

"It left the gate at 8 AM. It departed Newark at 8:40. Controllers in Cleveland lost contact moments ago."

Suddenly, a transmission came over the base radio that a flight attendant's husband was calling to report that his wife on board had said her plane had been hijacked. A moment later, at 9:35, Terri got a call that it was true: Flight 93 had been commandeered. Nobody knew any details.

Out the window, smoke rose high in the air as the Trade Center burned. "God give me strength," she thought. "Please, God, give us all strength."

At 10:03 she got a report that Flight 93 had crashed, and her heart sank. Rather than stop, however, she went to work. That's what she had been trained to do. She called all her managers together for a crisis meeting in the Red Carpet Club. She got out the crisis manual and began to read from it. "There were plans for how to handle a bomb on a plane, plans for a hijacking when the hijackers bring the plane back. A plan for a crash, but nothing for this," she said. They had never been given any warnings.

She turned to her boss, Tom McCabe, who had been there for the regular monthly meeting—an age earlier. Tom pitched in. He was quiet and competent. He took control of the crisis planning, which gave Terri an opportunity to return to her office. "Thank God for Tom," she said.

That moment she thought of her son. She was a single mom and her son, a teenager, would be at school. He would be worried for her. What should she do, how could she reassure him. And her dog, Samantha! She wouldn't be going home that night. Who would feed Samantha? All these thoughts cascaded on top of a million other ones.

"FBI on the line," said her secretary in her office. "It's Bill."

"I can't talk to him now," she said. Bill was the ranking FBI agent at the airport. She knew him well. They were friends, but she didn't have time for personal calls.

"He's called three times," said her secretary.

"I don't have time. Tell him I'll talk to him later," she said, adding, "I'm going down to the gates."

She walked along the long, glass corridor that ran from the screening station to the gates, the same path that the person or persons who had taken her plane, Flight 93, had walked.

"God give me strength," she repeated, as she walked. "Please, God. Please."

She walked toward Gate 17, the first gate on the left. She knew all her planes. Flight 93 had departed from Gate 17. She had seen it parked at the gate out her office window earlier that morning. Now she wanted to talk to her staff, to the agents who had boarded the passengers for Flight 93, when suddenly two burly customs agents appeared. They had severe looks on their faces.

"Terri Rizzuto?" said one.

"Yes."

"You're under arrest."

"What?"

"Interfering with a criminal investigation."

"What! What are you talking about?"

They told her about the three phone calls from the FBI she had refused to take.

Bill, she thought! He had not been calling to chat. He had been calling on official FBI business! She got him on the phone and apologized and soon things were cleared up. The FBI needed the plane's manifest, and the PNR, the Passengers' Name Report. That wasn't easy to do, she said, to get permission to release that, but she got it done. Then she walked to Gate 17 and approached a supervisor who handed her four boarding passes.

"What are these?" she said.

"The men, who did this maybe."

"What? How do you know?"

The superior pointed to a gate agent, one of the two agents who had boarded the flight. He was a long time gate agent, one of Terri's best. She walked over to talk to him. He was terribly shaken.

"How do you know?" she said.

"They were too well-dressed," he said.

"Too well-dressed."

"Too well-dressed for that early in the morning. And their muscles rippled below their suits."

"Their muscles?"

"Yes, and their eyes."

Terri's heart sank as she saw the pain in her agent's eyes at that moment. He was a long-time agent, one of her best, but this was America, and we did not prejudge people because they appeared too well-dressed, or because their muscles rippled under their suits, or for the self-absorbed look in their eyes.

This was America, but from that day on, that would be the agent's sorrow, as it would be all American's sorrow—now that the world that had been had turned.

BOOK *Two*

AFTER THAT DAY

Chapter Eleven

WHAT DO WE DO WITH THE SORROW?

P<small>LANES HAVE</small> always fascinated me. When I was a boy of ten or so, I'd come home after school and set up in front of the picture window of our split level on Long Island. I'd wait for the planes to pass overhead on their final approach to JFK, called Idlewild in those days. JFK was president. The Boeing 707 was brand new.

I'd point the binoculars in the direction of the horizon and wait for the tiny silver dots to appear in the sky. As the sleek new Boeing 707s crossed over our house, flying low like the arc on a Mickey Mantle home run, I'd read the logos on their tails, and that's how I first became acquainted with the big, broad, exciting world I anticipated was out there. A world I couldn't wait to explore.

I came out of college in 1971 at the height of the "1960s" wanting to be a teacher, inspired in part by my ideal image of the world. I believed in Faulkner's "eternal verities of the heart," the idea that man will not merely endure but will prevail. As a teacher I saw myself as a "facilitator." I had gained the knowledge, and it was my job to impart it. I took my first job in Boston's public schools. But after 9/11, all that changed. The events of that morning challenged my core beliefs about the essential goodness of man: if I could not understand how nineteen men could destroy other human beings so wantonly, how could I teach anyone anything?

In Toronto, where our plane had been diverted that morning, one of the papers ran a poem by William Butler Yeats. Asked to capture the horror of World War I, Yeats said it was "too big." In 1914, he wrote:

"I think it better that in times like these
"A poet keep his mouth shut, for in truth
"We have no gift to set a statesman right;
"He has had enough of meddling who can please
"A young girl in the indolence of her youth
"Or an old man upon a winter's night."

That said it all. It was "too big." The enormity was too great to process. Nearly two years passed, but still I stood mute, a teacher unable to open his mouth. I doubted if we could endure, let alone prevail. I was a teacher grappling with the unanswerable question, and looking for someone to lead me to the answer:

How do we forgive the unforgivable?

I couldn't let them go, the men who had done this. Nearly two years had passed, but still I couldn't let them go. I needed to know why.

The Panther Motel sits on A1A, on the left side of the road, the inter-coastal side, not the fancy beach side. It's a nondescript structure, two stories tall with a balcony overlooking a kidney shaped pool. There are a million Panther Motels in Florida, and this was the perfect spot for three guys with evil intent to hole up.

In late August 2001, three of the 9/11 hijackers, Mohammed Atta, Marwan Al-Shehhi, and Ziad Jarrah, rented room 12 on the second floor of the Panther Motel, next to the office. From the room, the three ran an extension cord to the motel office's Internet connection. There they used the connection to perform last minute calculations for a plan they were developing. They had stayed for a time at another motel up the road, doing the same thing with an extension cord, but the manager of that place had grown suspicious, thinking they might be ringing up long-distance charges on his phone, and he pulled the plug. They protested, especially Jarrah, who told the manager, "We're on a mission," but the manager wasn't buying their act, and he bounced them.

According to the *Miami Herald,* the trio moved up the street to the Panther Motel. The manager there, Richard Surma, was more accommodating. After the attacks, Surma said, "They seemed so nice." He was speaking of Jarrah, who had perfected an ingratiating manner with Americans. Mohammed Atta, on the other hand, had no interest in manners. I couldn't imagine anyone mistaking him for nice. One of the Broward County sheriffs deputies assigned to the Ft. Lauderdale airport, where I worked, offered to talk to my training program about going into a 7-Eleven in his neighborhood one night during the summer of 2001. As he waited in line in civilian clothes to pay for cigarettes, a short guy in front of him berated the cashier in a loud voice.

"Hey, pal," the deputy said to the guy. "Go easy on the young lady, ya hear."

The short guy turned and pointed a finger at the cop's nose. "I should kill you," he said.

At the time, the deputy thought the guy was just another Florida nutcase. Only later, after 9/11, did he realized it had been Atta.

In the summer of 2003 I drove up the coast from the Ft. Lauderdale airport to the Panther Motel during one of my trips to Florida. I was feeling a swirl of emotions and looking for an outlet. When I was young, five maybe, I had reached to touch a lit barbeque, but my father had stopped me.

"Never touch a hot stove," he had said. It was wise advice, counsel I had lived by generally, but now as the rage after 9/11 continued to seethe inside me, confusing me as much as it disturbed me, I felt compelled to reject that sage advice. I couldn't let them go.

I needed to touch the hot stove.

———————————

A week earlier I had been to a ballgame in Seattle with my daughter. We had a good relationship, my daughter and I. We could talk freely to each other. That had been true ever since she was a kid, and we played a game. On Fridays, she'd wait for me to come home from work, her face positioned in the window. As I pulled up in the car, she'd hop on her Strawberry Shortcake tricycle for our weekly trek to the corner store to pick up pizza. I'd walk and she'd talk, telling me all about her day at the pool or whatever it was she had done. It was a game we played—our game. She was in college two years after 9/11, but still we liked to do games together. One day during the summer of 2003, a bright, blue day, we sat at a Seattle Mariners game when I spotted a jet flying low overhead. I watched it angle toward the city, and something about its path, the light that played across its fuselage, resurrected a tightness in the middle of me. I watched it knife behind a skyscraper, and I felt my heart sink. I told my daughter that we had to leave.

"What?"

"We have to go, " I said.

"Why?"

"Because we do."

She complied, and though the Mariners were in the middle of a rally, we walked out of the stadium in silence.

The men who had checked into the Panther Motel had altered the rotation of the world. Gone was the levity. Now we lived a "If you see something, say something" existence. Now all the joy of public places had been leached out.

I sensed it anytime I walked through Penn Station in New York and passed people who averted their eyes if you smiled at them. I sensed it as I sat at airport concession counters around the country with the only sound coming from ESPN on the TV, and no conversation from the people squeezed in tight beside me. I sensed it one morning nearly two years after 9/11 as I stood under the covered porch at the Marriott hotel at Newark airport. I had stood in this space many times during the 1990s when I had come to Newark to offer my training classes, but now as I waited for the shuttle bus in the slanting sun of a new day, I saw something unfamiliar in the eyes of travelers: an absence of light? Some sipped coffee, others checked out their wingtips, while yet others stared straight ahead. Silence predominated, and I sensed that a chasm had been opened in our collected self-confidence by the events that had had their genesis under this porch. This is where the hijackers on Flight 93 had started their journey that morning, a journey that had been intended to turn us inward, away from each other.

Maybe it was just me, but I don't think so. This was more than New Yorkers being New Yorkers. I sensed an unspoken weariness had filled the void. Maybe it was the fatigue of up and down terror alerts, the debilitating drip, drip, drip of what might happen next. Maybe it was the awareness of long lines that awaited everyone once they got to the terminals, the unhappy prospect of packed planes and long flights stripped of all amenities, including peanuts. Or maybe it was something deeper.

Maybe it was the regret for lost intangibles.

I sensed the people around me were asking a question with their averted eyes, the same question I had been asking myself for nearly two years: how do we recover what's been lost? How do we take back our world from fear?

How do we reclaim the sky?

———————

Shoes clapping on the tile, I crossed the balcony to Room 12. There, I stood in front of a broad, flat window with a gray, sun-bleached curtain pulled tight against it. I could not see through the curtain, but in my mind's eye I imagined the men who had been at the center of the attacks working on a computer behind this screen. I could feel their energy. It was a powerful, negative energy, one that had not been diminished by time, even as the enormity of their crimes had not been diminished.

The bitterness rose inside of me as I thought of Atta, Al-Shehhi, and Jarrah putting the finishing touches on their "mission" in this space. I felt the tightness again. It was the same tightness I had felt at the game with my daughter. I had felt it for the first time in baggage claim in Toronto, the moment I had heard the word "fell" to describe the towers. Now, nearly two years later, it had not subsided but only grown more acute.

I have a friend, a fellow trainer named Janet Ott. She's the lead trainer for a group called Excellence Northwest, based in Bellingham, Washington. Janet is a diminutive woman with fiery red hair and blue eyes that look all the way to the back of your head. She served as an army nurse in Vietnam, where she tended to wounded soldiers during some of the fiercest fighting. Often she talks about the "tightness" that can consume the center of a person. It's an all-encompassing grip of emotions, she says, one she knew first hand, or as she said of her experience in Vietnam: "It took me ten years before I could begin to recover."

Janet has a theory that the choices we make in life lead to the results we get. If we make good choices, we move forward, part of what she calls "The Law of Attraction." The Law of Attraction states that we get back in life what we focus our energies on. If we focus on joy, we get joy. This is obvious, but when we focus on anger, we not only get more anger, we invite violence into our lives.

The violence can be overt, such as when we strike out at others, or it can be internal. Overt violence makes the news, but the internal form of violence is the violence we do to ourselves.

As I stood on the porch at the Panther, the tightness in my chest exacerbated by the hot sun, I understood the "mission" Jarrah had spoken about to the motel owner. I understood now why they had come: they had come to destroy directly, as many people as they could, but also to destroy indirectly. They wished to drive us away from life and from making connections with each other. They came to get us to inflict the internal form of violence on ourselves.

"You okay, Dad?" my daughter had said to me a week earlier as we had walked away from the game.

"Yeah," I said, "I'm fine." Then she said something that stayed with me, a comment that had prompted me to visit the Panther.

"What have they done to us all?" she asked.

Her comment stayed with me. As I stood on the porch at the Panther—staring at my reflection in the glass of Room 12—I knew the significance of this moment, and what I needed to do. No longer could I stand mute. My daughter had asked the key question. I had to find the answer.

For nearly twenty-years I had worked shoulder to shoulder with many of the aviation employees who had been centrally involved that morning, including those who worked at the three departure airports, Newark, Logan, and Dulles. My colleagues had come to work on the morning of September 11 expecting a routine day. Instead they found themselves in the middle of a national attack, one in which they had become the means. But though they had been so cynically abused, they had not flinched from their responsibilities. Cast in the role as first responders they had been equal to the challenge, and they had risen up.

That moment standing on the porch of the Panther I knew what I needed to do. I needed to go back to my friends and colleagues in aviation to ask them how they had been able to keep going in the face of such danger.

"What have they done to us all?" my daughter had asked, and I might not know the answer, but I knew where I was going to turn and to whom.

Where did you find the strength to keep going? I wanted to ask my friends and colleagues. How have you been able to prevail, rather than simply endure?

Chapter Twelve
TOM

Tom Innace grew up in a triple-decker house a few blocks away from the Flatbush Avenue subway station in Brooklyn. His aunt and uncle lived on the first floor of the tidy wooden structure, while his grandmother, a German immigrant who scrubbed floors for a living, occupied the second floor with her unmarried sister. Tom's mother and his father, who worked his entire life at the Shaeffer Brewery in Brooklyn, lived on the third floor where they raised their family, which sometimes included thirty children. That number is not a misprint.

"Most times we had four or five kids in the house," said Tom. "My folks took in children each time Catholic Charities called. Usually we had four or five kids at any given time, but all together we had about thirty."

Tom himself was one of the long parade of foster children from Catholic Charities who rotated through the family's two-bedroom third floor apartment during the fifties with two bedrooms and two storage rooms converted to bedrooms. "I was lucky," he said. "My parents never had two nickels to rub together, but they adopted me along the way, and so I had a regular roof."

Tom Innace is a Port Authority police officer who works out of Newark airport with Sue Baer. He's blonde with blue-eyes, hardly the picture of a cop who works a tough beat. He holds your gaze when he speaks, his voice soft. He's not at all a macho man. Asked why he became a Port Authority cop, he said, "I never forgot what was done for me."

The morning of 9/11, in the predawn darkness at Newark airport, Tom pitched in for an hour doing paperwork before hopping in a squad car and running over to a Port Authority office on Staten Island, beside the Goethal's Bridge toll plaza. He was there when somebody pointed to a TV on the wall and said, "Oh, man! Look at that!"

At first, Tom and two other officers watched silently, but only for a moment. Then they sprang into action. By the time the second plane hit, they were racing to the scene. "We drove like maniacs," he said.

Red light flashing, they rode the shoulder on the Jersey Turnpike and zipped into Manhattan through the Holland Tunnel. "We made it from Staten Island in about twelve minutes," he said.

They parked two blocks short of the South Tower and arrived at the police command center on West Street just as much of the horrific part was beginning—people were jumping from the highest floors of the towers.

The book, *102 Minutes: The Untold Story of the Fight to Survive Inside the Twin Towers,* by two *New York Times* reporters, Jim Dwyer and Kevin Flynn, tells how twenty-thousand people who had been trapped in the World Trade Center at the time of the attacks struggled to escape. Port Authority police played a key role, including Tom Innace.

He stood at the American Express Financial Center underneath the walkways to the Trade Center building, signaling to people to stop before rushing out of the Towers, shouting at the top of his lungs.

Debris continued to fall, including people who were jumping, and Tom—along with others—held people back in the Trade Center doorways, keeping them from dashing out blindly into the street and getting hit.

"Stop!" Tom would shout one moment. Then, when he could look up and see clear sky, he motioned furiously, bellowing, "Now. Go, go, go!"

Though he himself was threatened by debris as it fell, Tom focused on the people in the doorway, alternately holding his hand up, then waving like a pinwheel, "Okay. Now go, go, go! Run!"

"When the first tower came down, we had to push back," he said. "Then the second one came down, and we had to push back again."

Anna Quindlen, the *New York Times* columnist, wrote, "(That morning) is enshrined now in public memory as the last innocent morning in American life, before its people knew how much they were hated in the world, knew that home turf was no advantage, knew that the most invincible symbols of greatness were so vulnerable that they could be laid low in less time than it takes to read a newspaper."

As the buildings collapsed, Tom Innace pushed back, but all the time, covered in soot and dust, he continued to work, and in so doing he and his fellow police officers helped save lives.

Two days later, Tom returned to the scene, to the "Pile," as they called it, bringing supplies from Newark Airport with him. Ultimately, he was assigned to full-time duty on the relief effort, going wherever they sent him in a series of twelve-hour shifts that lasted a full year. He was happy to do it, all part of an attempt by him and other officers to serve fallen comrades, thirty-seven of them from the Port Authority Police Department, who had died. He did this because, as he said, he wanted to be "helpful." He did it despite the personal cost, the look in his daughter's eye when he returned home one night after months of late nights at the "Pile" and offered to help her with her homework. "Mommy does my homework with me," she said.

The pain of that came on top of all the other pains, yet still Tom endured. He kept working.

"But there was a more important lesson of that day, and it is infinitely more important that it be remembered," wrote Anna Quindlan. "That morning marked the triumph of our best selves: the impatient martyrs of the fire companies who hurried up the stairs, the grimy angels with blowtorches who cleared away the steel, the heavenly chorus of people whose hearts seemed to lift from their bodies to touch the suffering of others. People fell and people rose, and the last is the lesson."

Tom Innace rose, as did so many others I knew at Newark, Logan, and Dulles. I was not surprised, but I was curious.

"Where do you find the strength?" I asked Tom one day in 2003, after my visit to the Panther Motel.

"I don't know," he said. "You just keep working."

His comment triggered for me a recollection of a truism I had long known as a teacher: if you want to know someone, really know them, you need to look beyond their actions to the core beliefs that determine their choices. There you will find the essence of a person. There you'll find what inspires their actions.

Tom Innace and so many others I knew at Newark, Logan, and Dulles had acted bravely. But that was something for the newspapers. Newspapers reported on events, including depictions of brave actions. But I wanted to go deeper than that. I wanted to learn what core beliefs my friends and colleagues held that had allowed them to act bravely.

Standing on the porch of the Panther, thinking of my daughter's question ("What have they done to us all?"—but more importantly wanting to know how to "undo" the damage) I knew the scope of my "mission." Instead of my being the "teacher," the one with the knowledge, I needed to move to the receiving end and become the "student."

And I knew where I needed to begin. I needed to begin at the beginning, by calling on the woman who had given me my start in aviation.

Sue Baer.

Chapter Thirteen
SUE

I FIRST MET Sue Baer in the spring of 1990. She was the general manager of Customer and Marketing Services for the Port Authority, based at the Trade Center. A year earlier, I had been invited to Newark airport by Port Authority officials to develop a taxi training program for 1200 Newark and Elizabeth cab drivers. The airport had suffered through three taxi strikes in a month, and Port Authority officials, led by the manager of airport services, Dick Williams, hoped training would help. I adapted my "Miami Nice" program, a program I had created for Miami cabbies, and it worked. Taxi complaints at Newark dropped by half, and the strikes stopped. That's when Sue called, suggesting lunch.

"Do you think the taxi program can be expanded for all airport workers?" she asked, as we sat over Caesar salads at a Newark airport hotel. Customer service had not yet become fashionable. Certainly no airports were doing it, and she wanted to be the first. She looked down at her salad as she asked the question, but as soon as I began to speak, the moment I said, "Yes," she looked up, directly into my eyes, a laser-like stare.

A straight-shooter, I thought. I'd love to work for this lady.

And I did. She hired me, and beginning in 1991, I introduced "Airport Ambassadors" for JFK, LaGuardia, and Newark. And Sue and I became friends.

Sue Baer was the oldest of four children. Her family lived in Allentown, Pennsylvania in a modest neighborhood, proof that parents without means can teach their kids to set a goal and go for it. As a pre-teen, she babysat and worked odd jobs to save money for the "best" college.

"I'm going to Barnard," she announced one evening at dinner. Her family wanted her to go to school at Penn State, where she might have a more "normal" college experience, these being the late sixties and times of tumult, but she craved the excitement of an ivy league experience in New York City.

Sue majored in anthropology and following graduation in 1972, spent three years living in Panama. Upon returning to the states—into a tough climate for job-hunters—she was told that the Port Authority, which owned and operated the World Trade Center, was hiring.

"They wanted women who could type," she said. "I convinced them that after traveling on my own through South and Central America, I could take whatever they gave me."

On one of her first assignments, she was sent into the basement of the World Trade Center to conduct an automated pool dispatching system analysis. "A what?" she asked. "Should we get a man?" was the response, which rallied her, and for months she labored in the dark recesses of the World Trade Center's underground parking garages figuring out a better way to dispatch vehicles from the motor pool.

Soon word spread: Got a difficult job? Get Sue Baer.

Joe Vanacore, who at one time had directed Newark International Airport, urged Sue to apply for the position of his executive assistant. He had been asked to conduct a major restructuring, and he wanted her keen analytical mind on his team. She applied, with sixty others, and got the job. Those were the days, she said, "When the Port Authority wanted to do something, it did it. No notice, no telling people. They just did it. They weren't much into customer service."

Sue changed that. She created 800 numbers, and conducted surveys, asking the public: what do you think of us, how can we help you, what can we do to make our work better? Still in her twenties, she was making her mark, one that drew upon three principles that would become her hallmark: How do you operate more efficiently? How do you serve the customer? And, most critically, how do you support your people who do the work?

Promotions followed and one day she was invited to take the manager's job at the Lincoln Tunnel, which she did, becoming not only the first woman director, but also the tunnel's youngest-ever general manager.

"I was petrified," she said. "I didn't know how to run a tunnel."

Quickly, she figured it out. The key was not to run the tunnel herself, but to support the people who did. She hit on a management theory, one that became her mantra. It's called, "The What and the How." The Port Authority police had created the saying, and it worked this way. It was the captain's job to lay out the vision, to tell the troops "what" he wanted. Then, it was up to the troops to use their expertise and experience to figure "how" they could deliver on the captain's expectation.

Sue applied the principle with the tunnel workers, including those who cleaned the tile, and who kept the traffic flowing. "I simply told them I wanted clean tile and the traffic to flow," she said. Then she gave them the tools and the support they needed to figure out "how." Nevertheless, the tunnel remained a challenge, particularly as she found the Port Authority employees who made the facility function to be a "dispirited" group.

"They didn't think of themselves as these great people who ran one of the country's most fascinating enterprises," she said. "But here it was, for God's sake, the Lincoln Tunnel, the world's only three-tube underwater tunnel. It was built in 1937 and was the end point for the Lincoln Highway, the portal to America. I had to get them whipped up."

Most tunnels consist of two tubes—two lanes going each direction. With the three-tube Lincoln Tunnel, the center tube reverses, depending on the time of day and flow of traffic in or out of the city.

Come holiday time, Sue had an idea. She gathered a group and trekked through the tunnel to Manhattan, to the garment district, and bought up all the red shiny fabric she could.

Back at the tunnel, the maintenance guys used chicken wire to fasten the fabric around the length and breadth of the Port Authority's administration building like a giant ribbon. Others crafted a big bow and perched it on top, transforming the drab, concrete structure into a giant present at the entrance to the tunnel.

The photo made all the papers and proud employees brought their families out to see their place of work and take pictures. Sue had achieved her goal of getting her staff to believe in themselves. Shortly after that she was given the job of running the Port Authority Bus Terminal, with its 180,000 patrons a day.

Safety was a big issue. Indigent people slept in the terminal's stairwells, and the facility was perceived as unsavory. To address the safety issue, and also help people, Sue created a homeless program that got people out of the stairwells and into shelters. The program won awards for innovation, and the bus terminal's safety numbers jumped. By the mid 1980s, Bob Aaronson, the Port Authority's Director of Aviation enticed her to come to the World Trade Center and work in aviation. The offer appealed to her for two reasons. First, she had set her sights on running as large a facility as possible, an airport. But secondly, she had recently married, and Joe Martella, her husband, the Port Authority's chief of police at the World Trade Center, worked at the twin towers.

The 9/11 tragedy wasn't Sue's first brush with terror. Snow fell, but it did not stick on February 26, 1993 as Sue rose before dawn and rode the subway from the small apartment she shared with her husband, to her office on the 65th floor of Tower One.

Sue and Joe had talked about starting a family, but at this point, Sue had been tapped for "big things," and career exerted a pull. Sue's meetings ended at noon, and after signing several requisitions placed in front of her by her pregnant secretary, Camille Puso, she took an elevator down and crossed through the hallway to the Marriott's health club on the 22nd floor. She changed into aerobics clothes for a noon step class and was lacing up her Nikes when a muffled explosion interrupted the musak in the locker room.

"I thought it was a transformer," Sue said. But when she stepped into the hallway, she saw thick, black smoke curling in waves and smelled gasoline. This was no transformer.

An air vent emitted smoke in a section of hallway, and suddenly she knew this was bad. "Let's go!" she said to the group of women in the locker room. Some wanted to wait for more information, but Sue, ever the manager, would not hear of that. She led a troupe down the winding emergency staircase to the plaza between the two immense towers. Large crowds milled about in the frigid air, as snow continued to swirl.

Sue stood in the expanse of the plaza, dressed only in workout attire—no coat or hat—and surveyed the situation, her mind racing. Suddenly there came a sound, a whoosh, and a huge plate glass window, broken by people high up in the building in an attempt to release smoke, fell several feet behind her and exploded in a shower of crystal fragments.

I could be killed if I stand around out here, Sue thought to herself. Her next thought was of her husband, Joe.

Joe's office was in the basement and soon it became apparent, as smoke billowed from the depths of the towers, that the basement was the source of whatever had happened. Sue climbed a wall and found a man in a Port Authority uniform.

"Seen Joe?" she asked, but the man was moving quickly in an opposite direction, and all he could do was point in a general direction behind him.

That was a good sign, she decided, though she did not know at the time that the explosion in Parking Level 2 had occurred outside Joe's office. Sue also didn't know that the refrigerator the Marriott had set against the wall of the Port Authority's police command center had acted as a buffer, absorbing the shock of the exploding Ryder truck that was detonated by terrorists. She didn't know about the twisted wreck of Joe's office or his crushed chair, which he had vacated seconds earlier to pour a cup of coffee. She knew only that she had to keep pressing ahead, to find Joe.

Sue hugged the building as she tried to work her way toward the basement, peppering people she recognized for information. Finally she found a man who said he had talked to Joe. He said Joe and several other Port Authority police had crawled out of their office and were packing a van with equipment so they could move to another, less obstructed spot where they could set up a command center. Sue was relieved and could now focus her attention on her own staff, some sixty in number, many of whom had taken to the emergency stairways and were pouring from the smoking building.

Sue positioned herself by the revolving doors fronting West Street where a Port Authority maintenance man saw her shivering and gave her a dirty green parka. Finally Sue found Camille, who was distraught but safe, and Sue relaxed further before she herself was hustled away by police. They directed her to a subway station north of the complex, and she made her way home in her sooty sweats and the green parka.

At home, her phone was ringing. "Joe's okay," she told both sets of anxious parents after she was finally able to get her husband on the phone. The man she had met on the street outside the building had been correct. Joe was unhurt and working out of a temporary command center, where he planned to remain the rest of the night.

Later, I asked Sue if she ever thought of the implications, what it all meant?

"It was senseless," she replied. "Six people died that day. How can there be any point to that?"

"What did you learn?"

"I believe that when we are grieving, it is best to do (something)," she said.

Eight years, six months, and thirteen days later, Sue Baer would be tested again.

Chapter Fourteen
ONEKA, SUE, AND BERNIE

By the evening of 9/11, Newark International Airport had been cleared and terminals evacuated, all but for the forty or so people who had been stranded when their international flights were cancelled.

A NOTAM—or "Notice To Airmen"—is an airport's formal communiqué with the aviation industry. That evening, Sandy Carpenter, a Port Authority senior airside operations agent, punched the following message, a NOTAM, into her computer. Instantly, the electronic message appeared inside the cabin of any plane looking for news regarding the status at Newark: NEWARK AIRPORT REMAINS CLOSED UNTIL FURTHER NOTICE. WE REGRET THAT THERE IS NO ESTIMATE AS TO WHEN THE AIRPORT WILL OPEN. ACCESS TO THE AIRPORT IS CURRENTLY LIMITED TO EMPLOYEES WITH VALID PORT AUTHORITY AIRPORT ID'S ONLY.

The point of the NOTAM was clear: this is something we have never experienced before, so let's all stick together and figure out a way to get through this—together.

By midnight, the airport was quiet, eerily so. Planes sat empty on the tarmac, and the terminals lay still. The only sound was the clinking and clanking of cots as Port Authority staff erected make-shift beds, forty of them, for the international travelers. The travelers lay down for the night as Huntley Lawrence's landside staff and Gateway

Security agents provided water, food, and whatever else could be scrambled together.

Oneka Lupe was one of a hundred Gateway agents who contributed to the effort. A native of Guyana, Oneka had come to America when she was twelve, settling in East Orange, New Jersey, just outside Newark, with her mother. Her father remained home in Africa to continue at his job.

The morning of 9/11, Oneka had been sleeping after working a night shift when her uncle called with news of the attacks. She got dressed immediately and tried to catch a bus into work, but no busses were running on her route. She called her office, and a supervisor sent a van out to pick her up. Oneka worked tirelessly all day, especially during those first few hours when pandemonium reigned and passengers were most distraught.

"Some cried uncontrollably," she said. "Others wanted to know if their Broadway show was going to be cancelled. We had to take care of them all. We had no clue what might happen next. We heard rumors that a plane had been hijacked and was flying back to be crashed into the airport, but we didn't know. All we could do was stay calm. We told people to keep moving if they wanted to be safe."

That night, and for the next two nights, Oneka stayed at the airport, sleeping on a cot in a room with other co-workers. She wanted to be on hand in case anything else occurred. "In case," she said, "we were attacked again."

That first night the airport morphed into an armed camp as police took positions in front of the terminals with AK-47s and fighter jets patrolled the sky. In the early hours of the new day, Sue Baer told John Jacoby that she was going home. Nicky had begun kindergarten that week, and she wanted to see him, and her daughter, Elizabeth.

"Tomorrow's another day," she said, and John smiled, an ironic one. Theirs was a code that only two people who had been through as much as they had, for as many years as they had, could understand.

"Today is tomorrow," he said.

"Yes," she said. "Let's hope it's better than this."

She got in her car and drove the forty minutes back to Montclair as if in a daze. When she walked in the door Jenny, the kids' nanny, met her and told her the children were sleeping.

"Joe call yet?" Sue asked. Sue had not spoken to her husband in hours, not since early that afternoon when she had gotten through to him at the United Nations where he was working to secure the building.

"Still in the City," Jenny said, and Sue knew what that meant. Joe had left the Port Authority after the 1993 terrorist attack. He took a job as a security deputy for the UN, second in command for security in New York and second in command of the UN's peace-keeping missions abroad. Sue understood Joe would work through the night to secure the UN from possible attack; he had worked through the night in '93 also.

She went upstairs and gave each of her children a kiss. Then she took a shower with the idea of lying down for several hours, but as she lay in the stillness, all she could do was toss and turn. She did that for about ten minutes before she got up and got dressed. She went into the kitchen and wrote a note for Nicky's teacher. "Nicky will probably have questions," she said in the note, as she packed his lunch with tears in her eyes, "Please be patient with him."

She kissed her children one more time as they slept, gave Jenny a hug, and got back in the car. Again it was still, but this time she did not let the stillness disturb her. This time, as she navigated neighborhood back streets toward the highway, she let the calm of the night infuriate her. You will not break us, she thought as she pulled onto the highway and gained speed, heading straight as an arrow back to the airport, the job she had taken so she could help restore the glory days.

"You cannot beat us," she said to the open air and the windshield and the world out there. "We will not be beaten by you."

Dawn broke brilliantly, as it had one day earlier, but now the world outside Sue's office had turned dark. Still, Sue told her people not to be diminished by the actions that had been inflicted on them, actions that had been intended to do precisely that, to reduce them.

"When grieving, it is best to do something," she said in the early light of the new morning. "Find something you can do for somebody and do it. Nobody heals alone."

News filtered in, first as a trickle, then as a steady stream, including stories of friends and colleagues who had made it out, people such as Randy Saunders, who had served as one of Sue's assistants when she had been the manager at LaGuardia. Randy had been attending a meeting on one of the upper floors of the North Tower, above the point where the first plane had struck. He had guessed he would not survive, but he did, and he promised God that he would retire if he lived, because he had been trapped in the North Tower the first time, in 1993, when the terrorists had come. "I don't know how many more of these I have in me," he said.

There were others who had been brave, as well as lucky, such as the man from the Port Authority's planning department who walked down dozens of flights of stairs with a woman he did not know. He was an "anonymous hero," since nobody knew his name, but they knew his story, how he had remained with the woman from one of the Port Authority administrative areas after she found it difficult to keep going down the emergency stairs. "Go," she had said to the stranger, pointing to his wedding ring. "I don't have a family." But he refused, and instead helped her navigate down, and they had been one of the last to make it out across the lobby of the North Tower before it fell.

"Every time we heard about someone who got out, it was a gift," Sue said. They got another gift when Frank Loprano's secretary, Anne Leahy called. "I had a fight with a guard in the parking lot and missed my bus," she told Frank.

"Thank God!" he said, relieved.

That was like Anne, a spunky blonde, to fight with a guard. She was the kind to stand up for herself if she believed she was right. She had driven to Jersey City shortly past dawn to park in the Port Authority lot. She had planned to catch a bus to the World Trade Center so she could be at her class by 8 AM, but the guard at the gate told her she couldn't put her car in the lot. It was a big lot, with lots of open spaces,, and she had asked the guard, "Why not?"

Anne Leahy was feisty and was no easy pushover for a guard with an "attitude." But that morning she had met her match. The guard would not budge, and she had missed her bus. By the time she found a space she was on a later bus, which pulled up below the North Tower just as the first plane struck at 8:46 AM. Debris showered all around as the driver threw the bus into reverse, screaming at everyone, "Get down! Get down!" The rest of the morning became pandemonium, she told Frank, but he said a silent prayer, thankful that she was safe.

Trevor Liddle finally got a call, too. His wife, Laurie, had made it to the lobby of the North Tower—winding down eighty-three floors through a narrow staircase—just as the South Tower fell. She had been propelled to the ground and needed to climb through dust and darkness to get out, but she somehow made it to sunlight and fresh air, and then she had miraculously found a phone that worked.

But there were many other stories of friends and colleagues who did not get out or who were still listed as missing, stories of colleagues who had run upstairs to the upper levels of the North Tower with crowbars. As people ran down, they had run up, because that's how they saw their job, as a duty to help. With each passing hour, the lack of news about them became more ominous. By the time the final account was taken, days and weeks later, eighty-four Port Authority employees had lost their lives, including thirty-seven police officers.

One of those officers, Steve Huzcko, had called Sue the afternoon before, on September 10. A registered nurse as well as a police officer, Steve wanted to put defibrillators in all the terminals at Newark. On September 10, he had called Sue to see how he might get budget approval.

"How many you need?" she had asked him.

"Twenty maybe," said Steve.

"No, I mean how many do you *really* need, to do the job right. Don't worry about money."

"Forty-two," he said.

After 9/11, Steve's wife approached Sue. She told her how excited Steve had been at the dinner table the evening of September 10. "That's all he could talk about," she said, "how you gave him money to do the job right."

Since 9/11, four people have been saved at Newark airport following heart attacks because of Steve Huzcko's defibrillators.

————————

True to her word, whoever had an idea—something they imagined could be helpful—Sue supported them. When someone had an idea to feed people who had been stranded, she affirmed them. "Here," she said. "Take my credit card." When someone had an idea to get the people a shower, she said. "Get a bus. Take them over to the maintenance locker room." When someone else had an idea to check airport area hotels, to see if travelers there needed to get in touch with relatives, she said, "Do it."

Sue gave her people opportunities, believing that it's better to do something, even something small, than to sit in your office and think.

Nobody heals alone.

"Planes were not flying, at least not initially, but there *were* things to do," she said. "The gates around the perimeter needed to be checked. Locks on doors had to be changed. In the parking garages we were given a new rule that no car could be any closer than three hundred feet to any of the terminals. Someone had to make a plan. Get out into the field and look for things, I told my people. Find something to do for somebody and I'll approve it."

Later, the 9/11 Commission would ask Sue what she had known in advance. She went back to check all the security advisories she had received in the six months leading up to 9/11. None of the advisories contained any advanced warning.

"Nothing, nada, not a damn thing," she told the investigators "Whatever you saw on TV, that's all I got."

Rather than get angry, however, Sue turned her emotions into action. The country was floundering, but that didn't mean she couldn't do something. "We could take big things and break them into little tasks," she said. "And so we did. Focus and do, focus and do, I told my staff. This is everyone's tragedy."

She reminded her people of that the first morning, and every morning thereafter, but she knew also that she had a problem, a growing problem. "We never considered that we would have need for comfort ourselves. It never occurred to us that we would need a family assistance center for the Port Authority."

And so she turned to a man who had been working without a break. His name was Bernie Schettino, and he was an airside duty manager. Sue sought him out because Bernie had taken courses in counseling, and had studied several of the airlines' family assistance models. But most of all, she sought him out because she knew his character.

"Bernie?" Sue asked, as she encountered him in the hallway outside her office two days after 9/11. "Have you got a few more hours in you?"

"Whadya need?"

Bernie Schettino describes himself as a career guy. Tall, lanky, a former basketball player from Erasmus High School in Brooklyn, Bernie had been with the Port Authority for twenty-eight years. "I was a purchasing agent with a brokerage house when I got out of high school," he said. "Then the brokerage house merged with another brokerage house, and they found they had one too many purchasing agents."

Like a lot of guys from his generation, he learned about the Port Authority through word of mouth. "I heard you could get steady work and a chance for a college education," he said.

Bernie started with the tunnels, bridges, and terminals department (TB&T), as a facilities operations agent, and later was an agent at the Port Authority Bus Terminal before moving into aviation, where ultimately he became an airport duty manager, a key position at Newark Airport.

Bernie's job covered the airport's entire airfield operations and carried the responsibility of acting as a surrogate for the general manager in his or her absence.

The morning of 9/11, Bernie Schettino was home in Staten Island, sleeping after working the night shift. His wife woke him, and he turned on the television. As soon as he saw the news, he jumped in his car and drove in to work, riding the shoulder of the road to skirt traffic. Bernie had been working thirty hours straight by the time Sue approached him. She explained how families of the Port Authority were also victims of the World Trade Center tragedy and were dazed and confused. They had no place to turn.

"Happy to," he told Sue when she asked him to create an assistance center for Port Authority staff and their families. For the next five weeks—working eighteen-hour days without a day off—Bernie did what he always does, he led.

First, Bernie got the Newark Airport Marriott to give them a room. The Marriott provided phone lines and whatever else Bernie needed. He set up operations in the same area where Jarrah and his team of hijackers had walked, where they had dined in luxury the night before setting out on their destructive path. Bernie made the space work for Port Authority family members who came to the hotel, decimated and distraught.

"We did whatever we could for people," Bernie said, "It was incredible how people pitched in. The Red Cross was fantastic, but then you had retired police captains working the phones. Port Authority people who themselves had barely survived came in. Soot all over them, they went home, got cleaned up and came in to help their colleagues' families. We even had one maintenance guy whose father owned a pizza place in Elizabeth. He asked, 'You need food?' and I said, 'I guess,' and the next thing I know vans start pulling up with pizzas. It was the Port Authority's worst hour, and yet it was our finest hour—everybody will tell you that—the way our people rallied."

The greatest need, of course, was for information. Once family members received sad confirmation about the fate of a loved one, they needed information about insurance, benefits, and an entire host of administrative details that many had no idea about. Gary Davis, who was both the airport's director of operations, and a lawyer who provided legal assistance, joined Bernie.

Then, of course, there were some who remained in denial. "It broke your heart," said Bernie. "People didn't want to give up hope. On rainy days, they'd say, 'I'm glad for the rain, because that means my loved one will get water down there.' Others would ask for the plans for the World Trade Center. They'd say, 'My husband knows every nook and cranny of those buildings. Get me the plans, I'm sure he's found an area to climb into and wait.' "

Despite the training Bernie had gained taking courses and attending workshops with the airlines, there was no way to prepare for the challenges this event presented.

"You had to show them your heart," he said. "That's all you could do for people. We tried to show them our hearts."

Chapter Fifteen

THE DCA GATHERING PLACE

WHEN DEBBIE ROLAND arrived at Dulles airport in Washington at 8 AM the morning of September 12, she found that news in the American Airlines stations manager's office was sporadic and changing by the moment. Debbie's a "connector." She's got an address book that would make the Manhattan phone book look like a pamphlet. And she's always on the go. Often I'd get E-mails with her weekly schedule: MON, TO DALLAS. BACK TUE LATE. WED, IN DC, AT CONGRESS, SAFETY HEARING. THURS/FRI, A TURN TO LA. Her weekends were no less frenetic: SAT, SEE DAD. SUN, DO E-MAIL, CATCH UP, THEN CLEAN UP THE GARDEN. The focus of her effort was always outward—on others. The morning after 9/11, when she discovered that all flight attendants could get was an 800 number and a recording, she called her APFA base chairperson in Dallas.

"We need a place for our people," she told him.

"Go to the hotel where we lay-over. See what they can do for you," he said.

She went to the front desk and explained the situation. Instantly, four people appeared.

"What can we do for you?" asked the hotel manager.

"I need a room, a TV, outlets, phones, food."

"Right away," he said.

"And one more thing. No lawyers and no media."

The flight attendants called the hotel room the "DCA Gathering Place," the call letters DCA refer to Washington National Airport. The DCA Gathering Place became their safe place, a buffer against the loss.

Among the fifty-eight passengers who died on Flight 77 was M.J. Booth, the station manager's secretary. She had been heading out to Los Angeles for an employee credit union meeting. In addition, Rosemary Dillard had put her husband Eddie on Flight 77 in the predawn light that morning, dropping him off at the door at Dulles before continuing onto work at Reagan. Eddie, a retiree from RJ Reynolds, had planned to fly to Los Angeles to check on rental property the couple owned. Retired captain Bud Flagg and his wife Dee had also boarded Flight 77 that morning.

The DCA base is a small one, so the loss of M.J., Eddie, and the Flagg couple compounded the pain for this tight-knit group. They were also grieving for the four flight attendants who had been assigned to Flight 77, including Michelle Heidenberger, Renee May, and the married couple, Ken and Jennifer Lewis, along with the pilots, Chic Burlingame and David Charlebois. And, they worried about the hundreds of flight attendants who had been left stranded around the country. The morning of September 12 their families were calling the base at Dulles in panic, not only for word about their safety, but for news about their location and how to get in touch with them.

"Flight attendants are independent people, but when something needs to be done, everyone takes a share of the responsibility," said Debbie Roland, who with a dozen others helped create a "phone tree." Their goal was to get word out to flight attendants and pilots who had been stranded to let them know the DCA Gathering Place was open and available as a resource center.

The grief, palpable as it was, mixed with a powerful resentment over having been used. By training, but also by dint of personality, flight attendants are outgoing; they take the first step to meet the needs of others. On this day, a handful of men had played on those gracious qualities to turn their workplace into weapons—to use them and their profession to destroy others. The hurt and outrage ran deep. The phone tree group identified counselors and clergy who could come to the Gathering Place to provide support. From there, people and supplies poured in.

"It was spontaneous," Debbie said. "Somebody knew somebody who knew somebody else and, as the hours passed, people materialized. A nurse got a call from somebody telling her about our room, and she took the train up from Dallas. It was unbelievable. One moment we were stranded on an island all alone, then suddenly people started showing up, offering to help."

The room became a haven where they could comfort each other. Some brought their children because they didn't want to sit home, separated from their colleagues. Flight attendants set up rolls of paper on the floor for the kids who sat in circles with crayons and created banners. The group hung their work on the walls.

Part of the closeness people felt came from the nature of the job itself, a job unlike others for one simple reason: working in a cylinder at thirty-five thousand feet is not like working in a typical office.

"In an office, if you encounter a problem, generally you can at least try to get out," Debbie said. "We don't have that option, which is why we share a bond. 'Team' isn't just a concept with us. Team can mean life or death. The four we lost were some of the most competent flight attendants on our team."

The DCA Gathering Place offered this close-knit group an opportunity to share memories of their colleagues, including Michelle, Renee, Ken, and Jennifer.

"We all knew the flight crew," said Debbie. "We could imagine what our friends had experienced and could put ourselves in their places. It was natural for the mind to go in that direction, and that's why it was so crucial for us to be surrounded by friends who understood, and to honor these people we knew so well."

Linda Souder had been among the last to fly with the four flight attendants from Flight 77. The previous Saturday, September 8, she had flown home to DCA from Los Angeles with them. She had shared a jump seat with Michelle. "Michelle was a runner," Linda said. "Before boarding, she bought a chicken salad sandwich at the employee cafeteria. She asked me whether she should eat it, or eat the food on the plane. She decided to eat half of one and half of the other while she told me about her family, how well her two kids were doing in school. She had it together, that Michelle. She had life figured out. The power of final memories is fascinating, how perplexed she was over which sandwich to eat, mixed with the love for her kids."

Despite her busy schedule, including duties as a wife, mother, and flight attendant, Michelle Heidenberger had found time to volunteer at a home for unwed mothers and abused children near her home in Baltimore.

"The home, St. Ann's, gave her an outlet for her motherly instincts," said Toni Knisley. "Michelle told me how she loved to sit with the babies in a rocking chair."

"Michelle had the most engaging smile," Debbie added. "Whenever I saw her name on the schedule, I knew I'd see her walk through the door, and my day would be made."

Renee May, in her thirties, was "bubbly and funny," according to several flight attendants who reminisced about her.

"She had such a wry way of looking at things," said Debbie. "Where people might see stress on a flight—a missing coffee pot, a cart with a broken wheel, a cranky passenger—Renee always saw the humor."

"She had a wonderful high-pitched tone to her voice," said Linda Souder. "I loved listening to her. It was like having Judy Holiday on board a flight. I remember that last Saturday on the flight to Washington from L.A., how conscientious she was in the galley. She stacked the dishes so neatly. It's easy for me to see how she could be so brave on Tuesday, to call her dad to report details of what the hijackers were doing."

Ken and Jennifer Lewis were remembered for their adventurous spirit.

"Ken idolized Jennifer," said Debbie. "Anytime he and Jennifer got to a city after a flight, they would rent a car and go looking for 'adventures.' "

As word spread about the DCA Gathering Place, pilots stopped in to share memories. One pilot, a volunteer firefighter, had been off duty that day. He was at home when the alarm came in about a fire at the Pentagon, and he had rushed off to fight the blaze. He didn't know it was an American Airlines plane. The fire was so hot that it melted his mask.

"I came here for the comfort," he said.

Flight attendants kept the DCA Gathering Place going for five days, until the airspace reopened, and it was time to go back to work.

"Nobody thought of themselves as a hero," Debbie said. "If anything, we wanted to get back up in the air to show those who had taken our friends that they couldn't take any more from us."

Whether aviation employees thought of themselves as heroes or not, many acted bravely. Despite the worries of their family, they went back to work, flying in the dangerous skies, to get the country moving again. I often wonder if the general public gives them enough credit for that.

On Saturday, September 15, after the skies reopened, DCA flight attendants gathered with flowers at the Dulles American Airlines gates to await the arrival of flights coming in from around the country. When the first plane arrived from Los Angeles, the flight that would have been Flight 77 returning back to Dulles—Captain Terry Thames opened the cockpit window. He waved an American flag, and his colleagues jammed up against the concourse window and cheered. After that, a ramp agent, Jim Carlton, took it upon himself to greet every American Airlines flight arriving at a Dulles gate with a flag salute. He did that for more than a year, standing out on the tarmac, waving his flag, no matter what the weather. The flag now hangs in the National Museum of American History in Washington, DC.

The world continued to spin again after the DCA Gathering Place closed. The time came for memorials, and after that, time rushed forward, as it always does. The DCA Gathering Place had served its purpose. For a brief, fleeting moment, it had offered the comfort so many had sought. But it was not an easy comfort.

Toni Knisley told me about the first time she cried. It came six weeks after 9/11, on a trip to Gary, Indiana where she had driven with Rosemary Dillard to help with Eddie Dillard's funeral. One of Toni's childhood friends from southern Indiana drove up to meet her for lunch and, as Toni sat in a mall restaurant waiting for her friend to arrive, she felt a surge of emotion jump to the surface. She had been holding her emotions back for so long that the moment her friend appeared around the corner—the moment Toni saw her face—tears came gushing out.

"I have no idea what all those people in the mall must have thought," said Toni, "to see a grown woman simply break down. But it had been so long in coming, I couldn't hold it back."

Someone suggested they should keep the spirit of the DCA Gathering Place alive. "No one recalls who suggested it," said Debbie. "But we didn't forget it, either the spirit or the support we gained from each other."

Soon I would see proof of their resolve.

Chapter Sixteen
THE FIRST STEP

I CAUGHT SUE in the middle of a million things at Newark airport the day I called her during the summer of 2003, following my visit to the Panther. Since 9/11 she had many new challenges to deal with. Old worries persisted, including the most pressing, security, but new concerns, such as SARS and other illnesses, had been added to the on-going pressures she faced.

"Hi, Sue. Can I talk to you?" I asked.

"Sure," she said, typical Sue, straight from the hip. "What's up?"

"I've got a story idea."

"Oh?"

"I want to tell the story of the people from Newark, Logan, and Dulles who were in the middle of 9/11."

"What story?"

"I want to see if I can learn from them how to process loss and move toward recovery."

"When are you coming to town?"

"I'm here already."

"Come to the house," she said. "Seven o'clock. We're having a party for Jenny."

The string of strained relationships and broken dreams people had been going through since 9/11 played out in the media, but Sue was doing a formidable job. She was building back. As 2001 gave way to 2002, then to 2003, the fruit of her labors became clear: Newark airport showed a return to normalcy. Customer service ratings were up and complaints down. Despite the economic shocks that followed 9/11, Sue had found a way to prompt recovery.

What was her secret?

I drove up to Sue and Joe's house in Montclair, New Jersey on a July evening in 2003. Dressed in white shorts and a yellow tennis shirt, Sue waved hello with a spatula from the barbeque on the back porch. "Welcome!" she hollered, and I knew she would not allow herself to be deterred by sad thoughts, though they hung in the air. The Port Authority lost eighty-four people on 9/11, or as Sue said, "Nearly everyone was someone I could call by their first name."

But this was a birthday party for Jenny, the kids' nanny, and I knew Sue well enough to know there would be a celebration and a cake. A native of Jamaica, Jenny helped Sue prepare the picnic table on the porch before the sun set, as seven-year-old Nicky played on a jungle gym. Elizabeth, three, followed behind as Joe met me in the driveway with a "Murphy's Ale."

Joe Martela not only was a good cop, he was a pro. Tall and broad shouldered, with a manliness movie actors try to affect in their roles, Joe's job as second in command for security of the UN building in New York is a demanding job, but it has its benefits. When Pope John Paul II came to New York, Joe walked the Pontiff down a corridor in the UN basement to the restroom and chatted with the Holy Father, gaining a private audience, a big deal for an Italian Catholic boy from Jersey.

We sat around a circular table on the porch, and Joe started the prayer before signaling to Nicky to finish up. The wiry, bright-eyed boy made a garbled comment into his cupped hands, which prompted a touch from mom, and he righted the ship, earning a pat on his crew-cut head. We laughed and joked during dinner. When it was quiet and only Sue, Joe, and I remained at the table, she said, "So tell me about this idea you have."

"The intention of the hijackers was to shut America down," I said. "They used airports, including yours, to try to break this country."

"I know."

"What was it like for you that day?"

"It was horrific," she said. "Everyone saw it on TV. When the twin towers fell, we watched our home fall." She told the story about Steve Huzcko and the forty-two defibrillators. "We've saved lives with Steve's defibrillators."

"I'm afraid the further away you get from New York, Boston, and DC, the sense of deep sorrow drops off," I said, sharing a notion I had picked up traveling around the country. "I think sometimes people outside this immediate area consider what happened as if it happened to someone else."

Jenny returned to the table to clear dishes, and Sue got up to help. Joe and I sat across the table from each other, the silence engulfing us. I could feel Joe's pain as he sat with his arms folded, his eyes fixed over my shoulder, the sun gone and the twilight deepening.

"Let me see if I can help inside," he said, and he stood. I understood why he had to get up. Joe was no longer with the Port Authority Police Department, but many of the officers who had perished that day had been his men. I felt bad to have raised the issue with people who didn't think about 9/11 anymore. I watched Sue and Jenny through a window off the porch as they buzzed about in the yellow light of the kitchen. "I'll get the kids ready for bed," I heard Joe say through an open window, then a few minutes later Sue returned to the porch from the kitchen with a raspberry pie.

"Dessert?" she asked.

"Sure."

She cut the pie and handed me a plate. Then she sat back and curled her legs under her in her chair. It was now nearly dark, and fireflies flickered below a towering canopy of trees.

"What is it you're looking to do?" she said.

"My daughter asked me why this is so hard for people to get over. I'm trying to find the right answer to give her."

Sue knew my daughter, Caitlin. When Caitlin was small, Sue would let her hold the bowl with the prize letters at our annual Airport Ambassador award events. When Caitlin got older, Sue took her out in a Port Authority car to show her the airside at LaGuardia. Caitlin rode below the wings of huge planes, eyes wide. She loved Sue.

"Yes," Sue said. "Our kids need answers."

"How do you keep the anger from stopping you?" I asked.

"Anger doesn't work for me."

"They came to kill randomly, the bastards."

"I know, but anger doesn't work for me."

"Alienation, whatever religious veneer they want to put on it, doesn't give them the right to kill randomly."

"Are you angry?" she asked.

"No. I'm mad."

"What's the difference?"

"Anger gives them the victory they came for. I'll be damned if I'll do that, give them the satisfaction."

A moment passed, then she cut her pie, looking down as she spoke. "What can I do to help you?" I saw she was waiting for me to answer, but as I spoke, she looked up, directly into my eyes, with her laser-like stare.

"How do you do it?" I asked. "How do get your arms around the security? How do you stay strong?"

"We're Ops," she said. "That's what we do. We keep working. We soldier on."

I told her about Jeff Pearse's comment. Jeff, the former head of Patron Services at Newark, had set up the lunch meeting the day I had met Sue ten years earlier. "Jeff says he can't look at the Manhattan skyline any longer. All he sees is the hole."

"I know," she said, "all about the hole."

It wasn't until later, as I navigated the dark, deserted streets of downtown Elizabeth, driving around lost after failing to read the map Sue had drawn to help me get back to my hotel, that I realized the significance of her words. "Soldier on," she had said. Suddenly those simple words took on an entirely new level of meaning. If we hoped to prevail, not merely endure, we needed to find a way to deal with our anger. It wasn't a case of giving them satisfaction or not, it was about us. Finding a way to move forward.

As I pulled into the hotel parking lot, finding my way once again, I realized what Sue had given me. She had given me the first clue to recovery after loss:

Soldier on.

BOOK *Three*

CLUES TO RECOVERY

Chapter Seventeen
KATHRYN AND CHIC

Kᴀᴛʜʀʏɴ ʟᴇᴀʀɴᴇᴅ about the DCA Gathering Place from a colleague working the phone tree. When Kathryn arrived at the Gathering Place, she got right to work, doing whatever she could to pitch
in and help. By that point, two days after the attacks, the phone tree
had enlisted the aid of several counselors. Kathryn approached one of
the therapists and asked for help.

"I'm grateful I got the chance," she said. "I was lost, hurt, and
confused, like everyone else. I had been listening to the stories, everyone's recollections about our friends, and I was a mess. That was my
job, what I had been trained to do, to remain calm, but I was not doing a very good job. We sat down in a quiet place, and the counselor
waited for me to settle into my chair. Then she asked if I had known
anyone who had been on the plane. I mentioned Chic."

"Chic?" she asked.

"That's what we called the pilot, Charles Burlingame. I've known
him for years. We flew into Dulles from Los Angeles together the
night before."

"What is the special gift he gave you?" asked the therapist.

Kathryn stared back, head tilted. "Gift?" She hadn't thought of
it that way, that Chic had given her anything special, though they had
known each other for a long time. "I don't know if he gave me a gift."

"What do remember most about him?"

Kathryn smiled, a broad grin, since everyone knew this about Chic, it was no secret, "He was fast, always in a hurry."

"What do you mean?"

"Chic was always on the go." She told the therapist about occasions when a flight had departed late. "All the flight attendants had confidence. We knew Chic's talent, and nobody worried. We knew he'd bring us home on time. He had done that the night before, September 10, when we had flown in together."

"Really?" said the therapist, but she did not have to say more, in that instant Kathryn got her point, and understood.

"Wait," she said, "Now that I think about it . . ."

"Can you see the gift?"

"Yes!" she exclaimed.

Chic was telling her to slow down. "He's telling me to learn from him," Kathryn said. "He's telling me to take more time."

Kathryn knew she would think about this from that moment on. She would develop the thought and expand on it. "He's telling me to slow down, pay attention, take more time for people."

Chic Burlingame loved baseball, which is something I learned we had in common once I came to discover more about Chic from his friends at American Airlines. We were the same age too, something else we shared. I had been born in Los Angeles, but I had moved to New York just as Chic was moving into my old neighborhood in Orange County, California. As a boy, I had rooted for the Los Angeles Angels, which became his team. In fact, that's where he had been going on September 11, back to Los Angeles to celebrate his birthday at an Angel's baseball game with his brother. I felt closer to him, the more I knew about him.

Despite the similarities, however, we had different experiences that had shaped us growing up. I had gone to Woodstock and had watched The Who in the mud, while he had flown fighter jets on air-

Sue Baer, general manager of Newark Liberty International Airport, speaks at an airport memorial on the first anniversary of 9/11.

The Newark Liberty International Airport Airline Managers' Council raised funds for a memorial for Port Authority of NY and NJ employees who died on 9/11. Viewed from either direction, it spells out "9/11."

Port Authority airport duty manager, Bernie Schettino.

United Airlines training supervisor, Eileen Ammiano.

The "Glory Days": 1934 opening of Newark Airport's historic administration terminal building, which is now home to the Port Authority's aviation department at Newark.

Terri Rizzuto, the United Airlines station manager at Newark Airport, led her staff of 700 employees through the difficult days following the loss of UAL Flight 93.

Oneka Lupe, a Gateway Security agent, slept on a cot at Newark airport for days after 9/11 to be on hand to assist travelers.

Ed Freni (seated) and John Duval, senior operations officers for the Massachusetts Port Authority helped lead Logan Airport's response on 9/11 and in the pressure-filled weeks and months that followed.

Always With Us

UNITED

Marianne
MacFarlane

Jesus
Sanchez

Boston-based United Airlines customer service agents Maryanne MacFarlane and Jesus Sanchez were passengers on Flight 175.

Charles "Chic" Burlingame,
the captain of American Airlines
Flight 77.

Debbie Roland at Pentagon
Memorial Ceremony with
Captain John Darrah.

For more than a year after 9/11 Jim Carlton, an American Airlines ramp
agent, greeted flights at Washington's Dulles Airport with a flag salute.

Toni Knisley, left, with Rosemary Dillard and Sister Josephine at St. Ann's Infant and Maternity Home during the dedication of a videolibrary for Michelle Heidenberger.

Linda Souder, who was among the last to fly with her colleagues lost on Flight 77, works as a volunteer on troop flights.

Ken and Jennifer Lewis were called "Kennifer" by their American Airlines colleagues because they were known as "two peas in a pod."

Three hundred volunteers convened to create the "Kennifer Memorial Garden" in tribute to Ken and Jennifer Lewis.

A marble bench provides a focal point for visitors to the "Kennifer Memorial Garden" in Culpeper, Virginia.

craft carriers in the South China Sea. I wondered if I could ever truly know him. But from his devoted friends' stories, I believed I could. Yes, he had exhibited an eye for detail much greater than mine—while he used paint brushes to dust off the controls of his aircraft each time before departure, I had to buy new paint brushes each time I painted because I had failed to clean out the old ones—nevertheless, I responded to his character, and I found a connection with him there through my admiration for him. Chic Burlingame was responsible. He was a man accountable for his actions.

If Chic Burlingame told you he was going to do something, he did it, whether it was attending to his parents as they aged, volunteering for the naval reserve after he retired from the military, or sitting down behind the controls of an aircraft. If he took on a job, he did it with every ounce of his ability.

It was ironic that the army did not want Chic to be buried in his own plot in Arlington National Cemetery. The rules said that only Naval Reserve officers over the age of sixty could be buried in their own plot in Arlington. Chic Burlingame had been fifty-one, about to turn fifty-two on September 12, and did not qualify. Protests erupted, especially from veterans, many of whom offered to give up their own plots, but Senator John Warner of Virginia intervened, and the bureaucratic snafu was resolved. On December 13, 2001, Chic Burlingame was buried with honors at Arlington National Cemetery, but something important came out of the controversy. As a result, a key element of Chic Burlingame's character was revealed. When the FBI released a report of the forensic tests that had been performed on the bodies recovered from Flight 77, the tests proved that Captain Burlingame had not died in the crash. He had died *before* the crash. In other words, he had died fighting back, which is something his legion of friends at American Airlines could have told you. They knew the stuff Chic Burlingame was made of. Chic Burlingame would never have given up his plane without a fight.

"Chic always had the answers, but this one was bigger than he was," said his brother, Mark, at his burial ceremony. "I don't know what happened in that cockpit, but I'm sure they would have had to incapacitate him or kill him, because he would have done anything to prevent the kind of tragedy that befell that airplane."

Chic Burlingame died fighting back, and that made him an American hero. But he was a hero in another way, too. Chic epitomized values that have long marked this country, a drive for excellence, a commitment to hard work, and a devotion to duty. Chic died doing his duty. When asked if Chic Burlingame had ever seen enemy action during his time in the Navy, Perry Martini, his friend and fellow Annapolis grad, the president of their class in 1971, said, "Not until Tuesday."

Another Navy friend, Captain Barton Whitman, said, "To the forces of evil that took his life I say this to you: We are a nation of Chic Burlingames . . . you have taken this man from us, but his spirit is in tens of millions of Americans."

Kathryn got her first opportunity to apply the "gift" she felt she had received two weeks after 9/11 when she was assigned to a flight out of Dulles. Eager to refute the terrorists, American Airlines reintroduced the 8:10 AM flight from Dulles to Los Angeles as quickly as possible once the FAA reopened the skies. Kathryn was on board that September morning, her first flight out of Dulles again after the attacks.

It was an emotional day. One of Chic's close friends was in the cockpit as part of the flight crew. Plus, the passengers' unease was palpable, since danger still permeated the air. Barely two weeks had passed since four planes had been commandeered, including two American Airlines planes. The same security conditions, or lack of security, that terrorists had exploited were still in effect on Kathryn's flight. Were there more terrorists out there? Many people refused to fly, but flight attendants didn't have that luxury. They went back to work. They soldiered on.

As she strapped herself into a jump seat and departed Dulles on a Boeing 757 into another September sky, Kathryn wondered: might something else happen? Was there another shoe to drop? But as the plane ascended, she called upon the message she felt she had received from Chic. She put her anxieties aside and instead focused on her passengers' needs.

I had known Kathryn for twenty years, since my sister had invited her to our family's house for Thanksgiving one year in the early 1980's. She and my sister had met by coincidence—first they had met at a scuba diving class after both had moved to Washington as young career women just starting out ("I grew up in the midwest, of course, I'd want to scuba diving," Kathyrn said.). Then they discovered that they lived in apartment houses on the same block. Out of those twin encounters grew a life-long friendship. "There are no coincidences," Kathryn said at the Thanksgiving table that evening as a summation for the serendipity of her meeting my sister. That thought stayed with me, and not only had I been struck by her indomitably cheerful personality, but I had formed an impression of her as someone who saw beneath the surface of things.

Once I decided to explore the aviation side of the 9/11 story, I asked my sister if she thought Kathryn would be willing to talk to me.

"Call her," my sister said. "She's open as well as brave."

I called Kathryn at home one evening after she returned from a "turnaround" to Los Angeles, her regular route again. I asked if I could talk to her about Chic.

"Of course," she said, proving my sister's point. "Plus there are others from our DCA base you should meet."

"Why Chic?" I asked.

We sat at Kathryn's dining room table in her home in a quiet tree-lined street off Nebraska Avenue in Washington, DC. It was a gray day, a peaceful morning, made all the more calm by Kathryn's gentle manner. Beyond the window lay the garden where she had been sitting when she had first heard the news, that a plane had struck the

World Trade Center in New York. "My sanctuary," she called the garden. "That's where I go to reflect."

"Tell me about Chic," I said.

"He was responsible. I didn't know him as well as many of the others, but I always admired him."

"But why *that* gift, to take time?"

"I felt as if I was getting a message. I can't say really, except that I felt I should learn something."

Those who had commandeered Chic Burlingame's plane had come to turn us away from life, but Kathryn was refusing to do that. She was refusing to become an indirect victim of 9/11. Like Chic, she was fighting back. I had a key question, one that puzzled me.

"How are you able to keep your commitment in this environment?" I asked. Everyone knew about the aviation environment post 9/11. "Hassle bound," was the media's term for flying in a post 9/11 world. Those who worked in aviation faced hardships as well. Aviation employees who sold tickets, hauled the bags, or flew in the planes, including flight attendants and pilots, found themselves having to do more with less. Givebacks and cutbacks became the norm as their responsibilities increased. I wondered how Kathryn was able to keep her spirits up.

"It's not easy," she admitted.

Before 9/11, the airline kept a fourth flight attendant standing by at an airport to help in oversold situations. A single-aisle aircraft called for three flight attendants, but in the "old days," as many now referred to the period before 9/11, if a plane looked as if it might fill up, the flight service manager—Toni Knisley, for example—would assign a fourth flight attendant to help cover the load. After 9/11 that changed, as a flight attendant's responsibilities—including security responsibilities—increased. Or as the flight attendants put it, "Once meal service went, so went Number Four."

"I'm the floater among the three," said Kathryn. "One flight attendant stands in the back on a single-aisle plane, in the galley, while one works first class. As the floater, I help the flight attendant up front hang coats and get beverages before departure, then I hurry back and help passengers in the middle of the aircraft. That's our pressure point, crunch time, the final ten minutes before departure."

Flight attendants have always been trained to function as "first responders," but after 9/11, their duties in that regard became all the more critical. Kathryn talked about the pressures post 9/11, including new security responsibilities. No longer could passengers be presumed innocent. If a passenger loitered in an aisle, the flight attendant had to focus in, pay extra attention. They had to cast a wary eye on any action that appeared abnormal, while packed flights added to the customer service challenges of that job.

"The carry-on luggage has to be stored as we prepare for departure and overhead bins closed," Kathryn said. "Passengers need to be seated so we can close the door. If we don't depart on time, someone has to answer for that. You don't want to be *that* person, not in this economic environment."

"Pressure time for the floater, I'm sure."

"It doesn't sound like a big deal, balancing customer service and security, but the aircraft is full and people are crowding the aisle. You ask yourself, is the man lingering in the aisle suspect or merely inconsiderate? It's two minutes to departure, we're getting ready to close the door, and suddenly I'll see we're getting half a dozen late boardings—standbys and maybe a few wheelchairs. I'll smile and find space for everyone, but over my shoulder I'll see that passengers I've asked to turn off electronic equipment continue making cell phone calls. Then someone will need to use the bathroom at the same moment an unescorted minor asks for their grandma, usually at the moment an overhead bin won't close. Then comes an announcement from the cockpit, "Flight attendants prepare the cabin for departure." I'll see the gate agent standing by the door ready to close it, with their foot tapping, which I can't see, but I *know* it's tapping. That's when I remember my message—to take time for people."

"You keep smiling through all that?"

"I keep smiling because that's what I've promised myself to do."

"How?"

"I forgive," she said.

She said it like that, straight-out. The one thing that I could not do—for more than two years, I could not even speak the words—yet Kathryn had said it so simply: I forgive.

"Those who did this? You can forgive them?"

"Forgiveness is not about the other person. Forgiveness is about us. A choice I make."

"Why is forgiving the terrorists important before you can take time for people?"

"Because I need all my energy."

"I don't understand."

"I can't have negative energy. I need all my energy to be positive."

I looked across the table and I couldn't help but marvel at her calm. Kathryn was like clear water in a mountain stream. I was reminded of my initial impression of her as someone who saw beneath the surface of things. I glanced out the window to the garden, her "sanctuary." Possibly that's where she found calm, in her garden, a sanctuary that affirmed the certainty of cycles. Life's rejuvenating power. Whatever it was, wherever she got it, it worked for her.

"My last memory of Chic is so vivid," she said. "We were standing at the gate before getting on the plane in Los Angeles that Monday morning. He tapped his watch, 'Time to go, time to go,' he said. Then a day later he was gone. I had to learn something from this terrible thing. That's the gift."

I wasn't there yet, the forgiveness part, and I didn't know if I ever would be. There was no forgiveness in my heart, yet Kathryn had looked at a hero pilot's sacrifice and recognized the "gift" in it, something she could use to turn loss into hope.

Thanks to Kathryn, I had a new insight into the recovery process, a second clue—slow down, take time.

My sister had met Kathryn by accident. As a result I had met Kathryn.

Maybe there were no coincidences.

Chapter Eighteen
JOHN, ANNE, AND MARIANNE

A<small>T</small> 9:45 <small>ON THE</small> morning of 9/11, FAA National Operations Manager Ben Sliney, ordered all planes—all 3,949 of them in the air over the United States—to land immediately at the closest available airport. Never before in the history of aviation had the skies been cleared with a single order. It's interesting to note also that September 11, 2001 was Ben Sliney's first day on the job.

By 10 AM, planes were flying back to Logan from all directions, including some that had taken off from Boston, along with others in the vicinity that were looking for a place, any place, to put down.

"That morning we didn't know who was friend or foe," said John Duval, Logan's deputy director of operations. "All we could do was look up in the sky and pray." John gave an order to his Massport staff in the communications center, located on the sixth floor of the tower, to leave the building. If any planes flying back to Logan had destruction in mind, John figured they'd target the tower, and he didn't want his staff from the communication center, mostly young people, caught in that. Like Sue at Newark, neither John nor anyone at Massport had been given any advance warning.

John relocated his staff to the main building, while he, Ed Freni, and Joe Lawless, Massport's director of security, remained on the sixteenth floor of the tower and took the first step in their emergency plan: secure the airport.

"What might happen next?" he asked. "What else have we not anticipated?

By noon, Massport officials understood what they were dealing with. Four planes had crashed, but just as quickly, the wave of attacks stopped. Planes that had not responded to FAA requests to identify themselves during the height of the uncertainty, ultimately did call in, including Delta 1183 and others that John Duval had "worried about," but the question remained: despite the lull at midday, was this it?

In the terminals, flurries of activity continued into the afternoon. Bomb sniffing dogs would clear one area, then a call would come in about a bomb threat in another area, phoned in no doubt by a "copycatter." Each time a call came in, the dogs rushed off to that terminal, creating a stir. Later, as the lock-down continued and travelers, up to fifty thousand of them, were moved out of the airport, Ed Freni got a call from one of his staff at American.

"They found something," he was told.

It was Atta's suitcase. Atta had flown into Boston that morning on a USAir commuter flight from Portland, Maine. The flight had been late and Atta had rushed across from the USAir section in Terminal B. He had passed through the parking garage and across to the American Airlines area, but his bag had not made the connection to Flight 11. Inside, the FBI found a Koran, a pilot's wheel for training on a Boeing 767, and a change of clothes.

"My guess is he had the change of clothes with him so that if anything went wrong with the plan, he could change clothes and disappear into the crowd. These guys left nothing to chance," said Ed. "They had practiced for this."

Practiced, indeed.

There's the story of James Woods, the actor, who during the summer of 2001 had flown from Boston to Los Angeles on American Airlines Flight 11. The men seated around him in first class had caught his eye. They seemed introverted to the point of being boorish. He watched as they whispered among each other, and at the conclusion of the flight, Woods reported his concerns. But it was only after 9/11 that officials followed up and realized that the group Woods had identified were the same five men who had commandeered Flight 11 on September 11, 2001.

I spoke to flight attendants who told me the same thing—that they had seen Atta on flights out of Boston that summer. One even remembered serving him. The image stays with her. "His eyes," she said.

After the FBI processed Atta's bag, Duval's office got a call from a man who said he had had a fight that morning—a shouting match with "a car full of guys"—over a parking space. The man had not thought much about it, except to think the guys were crazy, until the events of the day unfolded, then he realized who they might have been.

That afternoon, John's team rushed over to the third level of the parking garage across from Terminal C, where the caller said he had encountered the men. There, John's team found a rental car and inside they found items similar to those discovered in Atta's suitcase. In addition to copies of the Koran and flight manuals, security found documents with names that matched the names Ed Freni had circled for United Flight 175.

For weeks following 9/11, John "lived" at the airport. The two planes that had struck the towers in New York had come from Boston. "Check and double check," John said. "Then check again. That's what drove us."

Finally, after he started coming home before midnight again, he would lie in bed and think about what needed to be accomplished next. One night when he couldn't sleep he got out of bed at 2 AM and drove back to the airport to do another perimeter check. He tested all the locks on all the aeronautical gates before returning home at 4 AM. Then he drove back to the airport to be at his desk by 6 AM. Check and double check, then check again. We talked regularly, John and I, following 9/11. I called him one day in 2003 to see how he was doing.

"Down to 173," he said.

"173?"

"Pounds. I'm down to 173 from 240."

Not bad for a guy who was nearing fifty. John had made a decision—if 9/11 didn't break him, then he was going to take control of the things he could. He worked out at a gym and even attended a "boot camp." He got his mile time down under seven minutes and his push-up regimen up to 100. His harbor-captain grandfather would have been proud.

"I have someone who wants to talk to you," John said to me on the phone one day. I had told him about talking to friends at Newark and Dulles, and I had asked him to keep an eye out for people at Logan Airport who were "soldiering on."

"Who?" I asked.

"Anne MacFarlane."

"Marianne's mom?" I remembered Marianne from the summer of 2001 when I had worked with Steve Bolognese to train United Airlines' agents.

Anne MacFarlane worked as a public information agent for Duval in his operations area. The "public infos" occupy booths in the terminals where they help travelers with transportation, lodging, and other needs. I had trained the public infos, but I didn't know Anne, since she had joined John's team after I had finished my sessions with that group in 2000.

"Anne said she'd like to talk to you," he said.

I had heard about Anne. On the afternoon of 9/11, families who had lost relatives and friends on the two airplanes that had departed from Logan, American Flight 11 and United 175, had rushed to the airport. There was a problem, though. Since airspace over the entire country was shut down, the airlines could not send their normal response teams, called "Go Teams" to Boston that morning, as they routinely do following an accident. Consequently, no family assistance center had yet been created.

So John and his staff took on the responsibility. Betty Desrosiers, one of John's fellow senior administrators, hurried in from maternity leave that afternoon and opened a family assistance center at the Hilton until airline staff could arrive. A woman from John's public information department joined Betty. Though the woman had only hours earlier learned that her daughter, a passenger aboard United Flight 175, had been lost, she still wanted to come in and help comfort others who had lost children.

Her name was Anne MacFarlane.

Chapter Nineteen
ANNE

JOHN SET up the meeting, and I stood outside the public info office waiting for Anne. When she turned the corner and smiled, I got the impression that's the kind of person she was, someone who took the first step to make another feel comfortable.

"John Duval said you're working on a story about hope," she said.

"Yes. Can I buy you a cup of coffee?"

"The benefit of working for Massport," she replied. "We get it free."

We sat across the lone table in the small break room under a fluorescent light and sipped our coffee. Medium height with a round, clear face and wide-set eyes, Anne wore a neat blue blazer, part of the public info uniform. As a personal touch she wore a pendant with Marianne's smiling photo on it. I recognized the curls instantly. Anne fingered the chain, letting the pendant dangle.

"Tell me about Marianne."

"She was my best friend. And I think I was hers, too."

———————

Marianne had loved aviation, according to Anne.

"She was a conscientious worker. One day, they—whoever 'they' were back then—hijacked a TWA plane in the desert. Do you remember that?"

"North Africa."

"It was a tense time, and Marianne was working the security checkpoint. That was her job before she joined the airlines. One day a man refused to open his bag. 'Can you open it, please,' she asked, but he told her he had a bomb in his case. Marianne was able to stay calm throughout. I've always been proud of her for that, though sometimes Marianne and I had our moments."

"How so?"

"We were both headstrong."

She told me about a whirlwind trip they took to Arizona.

"After we got there, Marianne said to me, 'Let's go see the Grand Canyon!' But it was the middle of the night, and I didn't like to drive after dark, so she suggested we go to Los Angeles, which seemed an okay idea, since I had a cousin there. We had visited him a few times when we had gone to L.A. to try to get on *The Price is Right*. This time we flew on a whim, but as my cousin wasn't home, we got on another plane and flew to San Francisco. We had a nice dinner at Fisherman's Wharf before coming home."

"Friends again?"

"Always," she said, before changing gears. "She was about to get her five year pin."

It was quiet as we sipped our coffee. The only sound was the buzzing of the fluorescent light.

"It never seemed strange to us," she said after a pause, "mother and daughter doing so many things together. We loved shopping. It didn't matter what the store was. If we passed it and the door was open, we went in. Sometimes we'd catch a plane, first flight out in the morning, and fly to Orlando. We'd get to the Contemporary Hotel by late morning and get our hair cut."

"At the Contemporary?"

"Always. We'd get lunch, do a little shopping, of course, and catch the evening flight home."

"How often did you do that?"

"Once a month maybe."

"Why?"

"To get our hair cut."

"Why go all the way to Orlando to get your hair cut?"

She looked at me like I had just dropped off the turnip truck.

"Both Marianne and I, we wouldn't let anyone other than Cindy at the Contemporary touch our curls."

As the time for Anne's shift approached, I asked if I could walk her to her station. She agreed, making the same motion with her head toward the door that I remembered Marianne making in class that day as she had headed out to round up stragglers. But what impressed me most was the way people were attracted to Anne, like steel filings to a magnet. She had a smile and a wave for everyone. In return, people of all ages had some piece of themselves they wanted to share with her. She was a connection-making machine!

"How do you do it?" I asked. "How do you keep going when you have lost so much?"

"Hugs and cups of coffee," she said.

"Hugs and coffee?"

"Everybody wants to give me hugs and buy me cups of coffee. Didn't you offer to buy me one?" I smiled, as we continued to walk. "But people do that as much for themselves as for me," she said, and I sensed a shift in her tone.

"What do you mean?"

"Other people need comfort as much as I do. What good is it to hold onto it?"

"Hold on to what?"

"The anger."

"Is that what they are doing?" I asked, trying to mask the discomfort I was feeling with the turn in the conversation.

"I see a lot of people who say we should get over 9/11. Let it go, they say. Turn the page, whatever expression they use. But they're not dealing with their anger. They're trying to bury it, and you can't do that."

"How do you know they're not dealing with it?"

"Because when they talk about 9/11, they wave their hand," she said, gesturing broadly, and I got the image of swatting at a fly.

"Is that what you do, give comfort?"

"That way, I don't have to wave *my* hand when I talk," she said. We came to her booth, but before I said good-bye, I asked if I could give her a hug.

"We already had the coffee, right?"

That afternoon as I walked away, turning back one last time for another look at this brave lady, another example of "soldiering on," I remembered from my studies with the Jesuits in high school that St. Francis said, "Teach. But only when necessary use words."

Here was a woman who through no fault of her own had been given a tremendous burden. Brutal men had taken the part of life most dear to her, but rather than turn inward, away from life, Anne MacFarlane had chosen a different response. She continued to make herself available to people, and in the process, she was giving me a new insight into recovery after loss—a third clue, this one around making connections.

By her example, she was teaching us all to get back out there onto the floor of life again. Make connections. Give and accept comfort.

Do hugs and cups of coffee.

No more swatting at flies.

Chapter Twenty

MARK, JOAN, AND STEVE

ONE HUNDRED thousand aviation employees lost their jobs in the first year after 9/11. As time progressed, the cuts and furloughs kept coming: tens of thousands more lost their jobs. The attacks roiled an industry that had been struggling for years with long-term structural issues of cost and capacity. The burden for dealing with the pressures of transitioning from the "old" to "something new" fell on the people who remained. Not only did they have to do more with less, but they carried the sorrow, the pain of lost colleagues, and the awareness that their industry had been used brutally as the means for the destruction.

Mark Hussey, United Airlines station manager in Boston, made an interesting comment to me one morning as we sat in the food court in Terminal C at Logan. We shared coffee before Mark had to go downstairs to work. Out the window the sun splashed across runways signaling the start of a new day, pressure-packed as it promised to be in our new, nervous world.

"In terms of recovering from 9/11, there's always been a tug between those who want to remember, and those who want to move on," he said.

Yes, I realized—that was it! That's what the "grapplers," the ten percent of the population that remains anxious "long after a calamity," as the World Health Organization describes it (me included!) wrestled with. The World Health Organization says that 50 percent of a population recovers quickly after a calamity. Forty percent recovers more slowly, but up to ten percent can remain anxious. That was the lot of the ten percent, to remain in a suspended state between contemplating loss and processing it. Those who wanted to "remember" had their hearts in the right place, but they had a liability too. If they kept too tight a focus on their grief, they ran the risk of getting "stuck." On the other hand, those who wanted to "move on" might, in their eagerness for progress, bury their emotions, and thus end up solving nothing. The "tug," as Mark called it, placed anyone who felt it in that tenuous middle ground that gave neither release or solace. Mark had put his finger on "grappler's angst."

"There must be a way to strike a balance," I said.

"The economics of the situation make that hard."

"How's that?" I was eager to get a station manager's perspective, especially one who had suffered on such a personal level.

"Before 9/11, organizations—I don't think it's limited to the airlines—believed they needed to focus on their people to run productively. The prevailing wisdom was that people should be regarded as a company's human assets."

"You did that. The dunk tank out front of Terminal C."

"I tried to. That's where I focused."

I nodded. This was management theory 101. Focusing on employees as "human assets" had been promoted throughout the second half of the 20th Century. No less a management guru than Peter Drucker had espoused the idea that motivated employees were the key to any corporation's success—and American business had concurred for generations.

"How's that changed?" I said.

"Since 9/11, the accent is less on people and more on creating a standardized system. Companies are looking to fit their people into a regimented model. Before 9/11, the thought was you should develop your people's individual talents. Now we take our supervisors to NASCAR."

"NASCAR?"

"Many corporations are doing it. Seven people work in the pit at NASCAR, where each person in the pit performs a highly standardized function. The cars roll in and the cars roll out, while each person in the pit performs a specific task to make the happen. The thought is if we can standardize the functions of the airline, from the curb to the seat on the plane, fit people to standardized tasks, then employees can be plugged in interchangeably."

"The passengers roll in, the passengers roll out. And now so do the employees?"

"It makes for an efficient model."

"But you lose the focus on the individual."

"That's the challenge."

"A brave new world."

"Competition is fierce. Everyone is trying to come up with an economic model that works."

"How do you feel about that?" I said.

Early on in his career Mark had been tapped as an "operational phenom," a guy with an uncanny approach to making the airline work, but he was also a guy who had spent his whole life developing people's individual talents.

"We'll make it work," he said.

Joan Twing grew up in Salem, Massachusetts. As a young girl she watched planes make big curving turns on final approach to Logan airport, and she always dreamed of working in aviation. She took a job at Logan in 1982. She worked for Eastern Airlines in their reservations department. It was a time when her two kids were small and working nights allowed her to have days to spend with them.

Then Eastern Airlines closed seven years later, and she walked across the airport to apply for a job, any job, at United Airlines.

"I had the seven year bug," she said. "That's what we say about aviation people, stay seven years and you're hooked for life."

She had been a teacher, and she became a trainer for United. That's how I met her, when I did my "Airport Ambassador" program for Steve and Mark. She was my "support." That word describes her perfectly. She always had a big smile. "Blithe spirit" comes to mind when describing Joan Twing.

Many of the customer service agents regarded her as a "favorite aunt," which was a term I heard often during the summer of 2001. "You can tell Joan anything," the agents would say. "Boyfriends, husbands, wives, hairstyles—Joan never judges."

9/11 was hard for Joan because it was so hard for the agents. "They used our station," Joan said. "They came here, into our home."

She did what she always did: she let people unload their burdens onto her, and she took a piece of their troubles on to her shoulders.

"Losing Marianne and Jesus was hard for everybody," she said. Aviation is not a job for everyone. It's a job of adjustments. You're always coming out of yourself to focus on the needs of others, and that's what Marianne and Jesus did so well. An agent might deal with five hundred people a day. That means coming out of yourself for strangers five hundred times daily. Marianne and Jesus never faltered. They did it, day in, day out. Everyone respected them for that."

Joan was among the first to meet Anne MacFarlane in the doorway of Terminal C when Anne came back to the airport that morning after dropping Marianne off.

"She knew," Joan said. "Nothing was official at that point, but she knew. I could see it in her face. All I could do was hug her."

The job didn't get any easier as time went on. From time to time agents who had dealt with the hijackers that morning would find Joan, to confide their lingering pain to her.

" 'The eyes,' one agent said to me. Over and over," Joan said. " 'It was their eyes.' "

"What did you tell her?" I asked Joan.

"What could I tell her? I told her not to blame herself. It wasn't her fault."

She was right. This was America. It wasn't the fault of an agent who had been trained, by me no less, to say, "Good morning. How can I help you?"

Rather than buckle under the pressure Joan decided to move in a new direction. She took a job with United that would allow her to make a positive change in her life.

"After seventeen years on the front line, I needed to take time, smell the flowers," she said. She took a job in the OZ office, which is where all the bills get paid, though her colleagues "upstairs" still call upon her for questions.

"9/11 taught me not to be afraid to try. It was a new challenge for me, to learn a new set of tasks. But that's what 9/11 taught me, don't be afraid to come out of your comfort zone. Never be afraid to try something new."

"We had three circles of employees who were hurting," Steve Bolognese told me when I met with him in the operations area at United. The world had changed certainly, but Americans were putting aside their fears of flying and returning to the skies. I wanted to hear from Steve his take on how the agents I had worked with were dealing with their sorrow, with the "tug" between "remembering" and "moving on?"

"In the third circle, we had everybody who worked at the station in Boston," he said. "We lost Marianne and Jesus. That affected everyone. In the second circle were those who had been on the floor that morning. Finally, in the first circle, were those who had had direct contact with the hijackers, employees who had worked the counters to check them in, or had worked the gate where Flight 175 had departed. They were the last ones to see the passengers before they got on the plane."

"How are they doing? The first circle?"

"One agent helped a couple fold up their car seat in the jetway that morning. He tagged the car seat for the father, while reassuring the mother it would be waiting on the other end. Then he waved good-bye and closed the door. How do you forget something like that?"

"You don't," I said. "How are they handling it?"

"Hard. Some have left the airline. Others have stayed. No one's gotten out unscathed."

"And you?"

"Ah, me," he said.

When I had worked with United that summer of 2001, the agents had looked to Steve as the "go to guy." If there were delays, flights that had been scheduled to arrive early in the evening, but had been pushed back to arrive in the wee hours of the morning, Steve would drive in from his home half an hour north to be there as the passengers—predictably disgruntled—got off their planes. He did it so the agents wouldn't have to do it alone. He was the guy "in the pinch," but this problem was "too big," which is how he put it, an expression that resonated with me: how do we forgive the unforgivable?

"This was something I couldn't fix," he said. "I always prided myself on my ability to solve problems. But this I couldn't solve. We all felt it, I know Mark did, that they had used our station. They had come onto our floor and took our plane. They walked in here and did it."

The pain cut deep. At a staff meeting shortly after the attacks, a United maintenance employee stood up at the back of the room and asked, "How could this have happened?"

"I knew the maintenance worker's frustration," Steve said. "But how do you explain to him, or anyone else for that matter, that this was a deliberate attack on our nation by people who do not have the same values or beliefs we do. It was a shift in the paradigm that shocked the world and caused the government to change its rules for security overnight. I could see that the maintenance guy was frustrated and hurt. We all were. What could I say?"

"What *did* you tell him?"

"I didn't," he said. "I buttoned my lip and kept silent."

He took a deep breath.

Indeed, prior to 9/11, it was widely reported that government allowed knives and blades of less than four inches on planes. After 9/11 all that changed . . . but none of that was comfort now.

"Part of the pain was the unknown," he said. "Our people wondered—could this happen again? Was United going to get hit another time? That was the feeling, the dread of the unknown, that they might try to finish us off. After the attacks, Massport started a daily 8:30 AM meeting. There John Duval, Ed Freni, and others shared the latest security information from all sources. They told us about the new security rules the government was creating, and how they planned to implement them all. I took that information and passed it onto our people. You look for little things you can do. That I could do. I could communicate with our people."

"What's the hardest part of it?" I said.

He showed me a letter from a customer that had come in shortly after 9/11. It was waiting for him when he had arrived back in Boston from Chicago, where he had been stranded.

The letter was addressed to "United's Customer Service Manager at Logan," and had found its way to his desk. The writer began by saying that he never wrote letters like this. "But the exceptional service I received from one of your employees on Saturday, September 8, 2001, was so outstanding I could not let the opportunity pass without mentioning him." The man concluded the letter by asking Steve to extend his personal thanks to the agent who had helped him that Saturday. "The young man's name," said the writer, "is Jesus Sanchez."

"That's the hardest part," Steve repeated. "The deliberate quality of what they did."

He handed me a button. It was a button that Joan Twing had produced to help raise funds for the MacFarlane and Sanchez families. On the button were the smiling faces of Marianne and Jesus, with the words, "Always with us."

"What do you do with the anger?" I asked.

"Are you angry?" I asked.

"Of course I'm angry."

"I use it to motivate me."

"Motivate you?"

"I remind myself how good my people are."

He didn't say how good my people "were," including Marianne and Jesus. He said, "are."

Soldiering on.

Chapter Twenty-One
UNSUNG HEROES

On the morning of 9/11, five of Terri Rizzuto's United Airlines ramp and maintenance employees went looking for a flag. You can't just buy a big flag at Newark airport—not one big enough for the job these guys had in mind—so they had to "find" one. They did, (or as Terri said later, "I don't want to know where they got it,") the five of them, Scott Mathews, Mike Fyfe, Pat Hofschneider, Steven Bloyed, and Rich Creighton, brought the flag up to Gate 17. The order had been given by the FAA and Ben Sliney to land all planes, the same order that had swelled the skies around Logan. Soon there would be a jet pulling up to Gate 17, but at that moment the gate was not being used. The five agents took advantage and walked down the jetway, with Mike Fyfe carrying the flag they had "found."

The long tubular corridor of the jetway ended in an open space. A blue sky, soft breeze and the sweet smell of the warm morning air greeted them as they arrived at the opening. They paused to look out over the sunlit tarmac, then Mike climbed up the side of the jetway. With one hand, he held the rail—as his colleagues steadied him below—and he used his other hand to jam the American flag into place. He found a bar at the top of the jetway where he could wedge the flag and get it to fit snugly, then he hopped down.

"Good," the four below said in unison.

Slowly, the flag flapped in the soft breeze of the morning, offering a steady pop-pop-pop as the wind began to catch it. The five stepped back and regarded their work. This was all very much against the rules, "finding" a flag like this, but their act spoke for everyone at United's Newark station. Their action said to those who had taken their plane and their friends and the lives of innocent passengers: you will not beat us! You cannot defeat us.

The message was clear and unequivocal, as clear as the breeze snapping the flag in the morning light: we will not submit to you.

United Airlines customer service agents at Newark carried a twin sorrow: not only had Flight 93 been their plane, but the crew had been Newark based. The pilots, Jason Dahl and Leroy Homer, and the flight attendants, Lorraine Bay, Sandra Bradshaw, Wanda Green, CeeCee Lyles, and Deborah Welsh, had passed in and out of the station regularly.

For nearly thirty years, Eileen Ammiano, a spunky blonde, worked as a United flight attendant based at Newark. Jersey-born and raised, Eileen had started her career at Newark because it was a "known," location close to home. But as time went on, and she received offers to transfer to other bases—invitations that offered opportunities for advancement—she declined them all, because, as she said, "I loved working out of Newark."

"It was all about our community of flight attendants," she said. When she began her career at Newark, United had 300 flight attendants stationed at EWR, the name for the Newark base. As United's presence at Newark expanded, that number grew to nearly a thousand by 2001, but "still we remained a tight-knit community," said Eileen.

In 1997, Eileen left flying to become a training supervisor. As a seasoned veteran, it was her job to fly on planes with new flight attendants and observe them. After the flight she would sit with the new recruits and go over things they did right, making constructive suggestions about things they might do differently.

"It was very positive," she said. "Our goal with the program was to support our new people. As our base expanded, we had a lot of flight attendants coming into the industry from other kinds of work, banking, retail or real estate. It was my job to orient them, help them achieve an easy transition.

On 9/11, Eileen had been assigned to fly to the west coast to provide support for a new group of flight attendants. She came into the station early that morning, because there were two flights to San Francisco that had new recruits assigned to work the flights, and she wanted to assess who needed her help the most. CeeCee Lyles had recently joined United after a career in law enforcement. She was scheduled to go out first that morning, on the 8AM departure, Flight 93. That morning, Eileen sat with CeeCee in the flight services office having coffee and making an assessment of CeeCee's needs.

"I was very impressed with how bright and energetic she was," Eileen said. "We chatted and the more we talked I realized that CeeCee would be OK on her own. She was flying with a first rate crew, some of our best flight attendants, and that plus how competent she appeared made me realize that the two flight attendants scheduled to go out on the afternoon flight needed my support more. I wanted to consider the first flight, I admit, for my own needs, going out later meant a longer day for me, but CeeCee was just too good. She didn't need me, and after we finished our coffee, I said good-bye. She headed out to Flight 93, and I made a call to schedule myself for the one o'clock."

The "What ifs" stay with Eileen in a powerful way.

"We knew nothing in the immediate hours afterward," she said. "All we knew was that we had lost a plane and that our colleagues were on that plane. I did what I could. Since I was the ranking flight services supervisor at the station that morning—since I had come in early to see CeeCee—I parceled out responsibilities. We started contacting family members of the crew. I worked nonstop. It's what kept me going. Thinking what I could do. I did that so I would not have to think about the what if."

The "What if" doesn't go away. Rather than succumb to it, however, Eileen threw herself into even more action. In the weeks and months following 9/11, she joined with Judee Beyer, the vice-president of CAUSE, the charity organization that supports United flight attendants, to help the Newark base raise money for a memorial for their colleagues lost on Flight 93.

"I remember CeeCee's eyes that morning," Eileen said. "My memory of her bright, eager eyes, motivated me to work on the Memorial. I had to do something. The enormity, it was too much to bear. But if there's one thing that sustained me, gave me strength, it was our community at EWR. My friends pulled me through."

Terri Rizzuto participated in a drive to raise money for a memorial for Port Authority in gratitude not only the PA loses, but in recognition for all that the Port Authority, including Sue Baer's staff, had done for the airlines.

The memorial, a large Roman numeral X, and a large I backed by the same numerals, was contributed by the Newark Liberty International Airport Airline Association Council (NIAAMCO) and erected in the courtyard of the Port Authority's refurbished old administration building, which Sue's aviation staff had moved into several months after 9/11. The symbols were commemorated in the courtyard on the first anniversary of 9/11. When viewed from any direction, either from the front or the back, the chrome numerals reflect the sun and spell out "Nine" and "Eleven." Earlier that year, in another gesture to salute the heroes of 9/11, the name of the airport was changed from "Newark International" to "Newark Liberty International."

One day when I was at Newark I bumped into Henry Carl, a terminal supervisor in the Port Authority's new offices in the refurbished administration building. Henry was one of the Port Authority officials I used to coordinate with when I'd come to Newark to offer training in the 1990s.

"Henry, I hear the airport put up a sign, a way to recognize the passengers on Flight 93. You know anything about that?"

"Yeah, they put up a big sign the day they changed the airport's name."

"Think I could see it?" The ceremony to change the name had been held in May, 2002. I wanted to see the new sign, to see the word "Liberty" spelled out.

"Let's take a ride," Henry said, and he drove me along the perimeter road to a long-term parking lot fronting the New Jersey Turnpike. There it was, a huge blue sign that read: NEWARK LIBERTY INTERNATIONAL AIRPORT.

"They had dignitaries out here when they put this sign up," said Henry. "And family members of the people on the flight. Following this one, we put up other signs along the roadways. Then we put signs up on the busses and terminal walls. Even the letterhead at the airport got changed. Everything has been changed to remember the heroes."

I looked out at the New Jersey Turnpike, and the cars whizzing past. This was the blue sign that had started it all, the first step in a formal effort to remember the heroes at Newark. I didn't know how many cars passed the airport each year, but I guessed it was in the millions. As they sped by, I wondered if people thought consciously about the word "Liberty," and what this sign represented. I had to believe the point was being made that a small, brave group of citizens on flight 93 had stood up for us all. I trusted that some day a child in the backseat of a car would look at this sign and ask mom or dad, "Why is the airport called Liberty?"

The sign was reminding us that we should never forget.

———————

While at Newark on a trip, I attended a farewell party at United for Terri Rizzuto. After many months of working nonstop to return her station to normality, Terri got an invitation to join her family's business, and she accepted.

The weeks and months immediately following 9/11 had been very taxing for Terri. She was pulled in countless ways. A supportive person by nature, she wanted to give her all to everyone, to the police and federal investigators with a million questions who "lived" at her station—in her office—and to her people, who labored under the sorrow of losing colleagues, as well as to the passengers who wanted to be reassured. As the company sent down requirements for cuts, mandated by the bankruptcy court which oversaw United's operations after it filed for Chapter 11 in the wake of the attacks, Terri never let anyone get a layoff notice without personally sitting down with them to explain why.

"I began my career on the ramp," she said. "I had always made it a point to know my people on a personal level. Once a month I would work the midnight shift, so I could get to know the people a manager who works days never gets to see. How could I not be with them when the pain of the cuts came down?"

A pilot wrote an anonymous E-mail to his pilot colleagues at United shortly after 9/11. It went out through the whole system. He had been piloting a plane that had been called back from the tarmac on the morning of 9/11. He had been third in line to take off when Sue had closed the airport. He had watched the towers burn from the runway. The evening before he had flown into Newark with Jason Dahl, the pilot who would captain Flight 93. Rather than paraphrase, here's what he wrote to his thousands of colleagues:

"Upon arrival in Ops, the magnitude of the events we had just witnessed from the front row was becoming evident. Ops told us that UAL Flight 175 was missing, and possibly another UAL flight also. As time went by, we learned this second plane was the plane Jason Dahl had been flying.

"I organized the stranded pilots in EWR . . . then I introduced myself to the EWR station manager, who quickly took me in as part of the EWR command center team. The next three days showed me more than the last 16 years at UAL. I watched first-hand a station manager that has to be one of the best, if not *the* best. Her group, though experiencing the same emotions as all Americans, and in many ways hurting more, continued to function, and well. They took care of each other, AND our passengers. They cared!

"I spent three days seeing the absolute best of the people at UAL."

———————

Terri's farewell—held in the Ops area under the gates—was a warm affair, "a good ole Italian party," said her mom, who drove in from El-mont, a suburb on Long Island just beyond the borough of Queens, with her dad. Her mom told stories about Terri as a young girl.

"You couldn't get her in the house with only one holler," she said.

Terri smiled to hear herself described that way. But it was true, she had grown up playing with the boys. She had learned that when you fell down and scraped your knees you picked yourself up and got back into the game.

A hand-made poster shone down on the group. There were photos taped to it, pictures of the pilots and flight attendants who had died on Flight 93. The pictures were different sizes and shapes, taken at the beach, at barbeques and at birthday celebrations. Staff had hung the poster immediately after 9/11, and time had curled the pictures at the edges. But the images still projected a powerful presence. We are with you, the message said. The response, unspoken, was no less emphatic. You are not forgotten.

When it came time for speeches, one of the ramp guys, the same group that had put up the flag, pulled out a box of earrings from Tiffany's. The guys had gone to Fifth Avenue in Manhattan them-selves to pick out the earrings in the turquoise box with the pink rib-bon.

"You're the best, and we want you to look the part," said one of the guys, a burly maintenance worker in overalls.

Terri opened her arms to give him a big hug. He accepted.

Chapter Twenty-Two
DIRT THERAPY

I GAINED a fourth clue to recovery beginning with an E-mail message I received from Debbie Roland, part of her outreach to six hundred people on her E-mail list: ANY MEMBERS OF THE DCA BASE WHO WANT TO CONTRIBUTE TO THE TOY DRIVE AT ST. ANN'S, LET ME KNOW, the message read. St, Ann's, I learned, is a home for unwed mothers and abused children in Baltimore.

"We are supporting a toy drive at St. Ann's every year to honor Michelle Heidenberger," Debbie said in response to my query asking for more information. "After we closed the DCA Gathering Place, our group made a commitment to keep the spirit of the room alive by doing charity projects."

I sent a check for $50, and got back another E-mail a week later with the following message: YOUR $50 BOUGHT A BALTIMORE ORIOLES CAP, A BOX OF LINCOLN LOGS, THE GAME CANDYLAND, TWO BARBIES, SIX BOXES OF CRAYONS, AND A YELLOWSTONE NATIONAL PARK COLORING BOOK.

This piqued my interest further, building as it did on the theme I had seen at United at Newark where people were directing their energies into charity projects to remember their friends. I called Debbie. She is busy not only with her work as a flight attendant, but with her duties as a union rep, and her work with various committees on in-flight safety. In addition, she serves as a member of the Wings Foundation, Inc. Board of Directors, a nonprofit organization that offers assistance to American Airlines flight attendants in times of distress.

"Can you tell me more about the toy drive?" I asked.

"Michelle used to volunteer at St. Ann's, so we support their toy drive each year to keep her memory alive for the kids. We all participate, but it was Toni Knisley's idea," she said. "Toni is a fountain of great ideas."

Toni, I learned, had been the "glue" that held the station in Washington together after the attacks. That morning she had remained by Rosemary Dillard's side, after Rosemary learned that her husband, Eddie, had been a passenger on Flight 77. Then she had followed the American Airlines station manager out to Dulles, at his direction. She had driven at eighty or ninety miles an hour, following an assortment of official cars back to Dulles, where the FBI—and a long night of investigations—awaited. After that, it was Toni who coordinated the memorials at the airport, and comforted family members of the flight attendants—as well as helping Rosemary with preparations for Eddie's funeral.

I called Toni, whom I knew would have all the details on the charity project at St. Ann's. More than that, I was to learn how the St. Ann's project idea came about. One day before Christmas, 2000, Michelle had stopped by Toni's office (at Ronald Reagan Washington National Airport) before taking a turn to Dallas.

"That was her custom," Toni said. "She'd pop her head in and say hello in the morning."

The two began talking about Christmas, and Michelle asked Toni if she should pick up teddy bears for the kids at St. Ann's. Earlier, someone at Michelle's church had mentioned that St. Ann's needed volunteers, and Michelle had volunteered at the children's home. "I rock the babies and feed them," she told Toni proudly.

"That's nice," said Toni, and she took a call. It can get hectic in the morning as the phones begin ringing off the hook.

"But the kids never get toys," Michelle continued. "What do you think about teddy bears?"

"I don't know about teddy bears," said Toni as she took another call. It's hard to concentrate on casual conversation when you've got to get flights out. "Teddy bears sound good. Who doesn't love a teddy bear?" Michelle waved good-bye, a big pinwheel of a wave, as Toni signaled good-bye and took yet another call.

After 9/11, people from around the country sent teddy bears to Washington, DC, in sympathy for the flight attendants who had been lost on Flight 77. The teddy bears came addressed to American Airlines, Washington, DC, but for some reason they all ended up in Toni's office, boxes and boxes of them. There are no coincidences, as Kathryn would say.

"You wouldn't believe how many teddy bears I got," Toni said. "From Bogotá, Bavaria, and Baton Rouge. Teddy bears piled floor to ceiling."

Toni didn't have to think about what to do with them. As Christmas 2001 drew near, Toni rented a truck, loaded up the teddy bears, and drove to St. Ann's to meet with Sister Francine, who had been Michelle's contact at the home. Sister Francine offered to take Toni on a tour, which concluded in the recreation hall, where Sister Francine pointed to an empty bookcase.

"Michelle wanted to fill that case with videos for the children," she said.

Toni could hardly restrain herself as she let out a "Ringee Ding!"

"Excuse me?" asked the sister.

"You just gave me an idea for our next DCA Gathering Place project."

Flight attendants from the DCA base began work on the St. Ann's video project in March 2002. Before it was over, the group had enlisted enough support—including cash and contributions—to present the kids at St. Ann's with a rocking chair, toy boxes, more stuffed animals, a TV, VCR, and DVD player, and a video library with more than a thousand titles.

"We made an event out of it," said Debbie, speaking for other members of the team who led the effort, including Michelle Smith, one of Michelle Heidenberger's closest friends and her regular flying companion. "We set aside sections in our homes to receive it all, piles of videos that rose to the ceiling."

By the time they were finished, the once barren recreation hall had been made into a screening room big enough to make a Hollywood mogul blush. But the team didn't stop there. After the video project, Toni got another idea. She got a call from a flight attendant who wanted to know if it would be okay to raise money to plant a tree in a park in Culpeper, Virginia as a tribute to Ken and Jennifer Lewis who had lived in the town.

"Sure," said Toni, but later, after she learned how important the environment had been to Ken and Jennifer, it occurred to her that something "bigger" might be better. One day she drove out to talk to the city manager in Culpeper, a small town two hours outside Washington, DC. He told her how much Ken and Jennifer had loved Yowell Park.

"That gave me the idea to do this on a grand scale," said Toni. "It was the summer of 2002, and we had the experience of the video library under our belt." Toni sent an E-mail to the other DCA flight attendants asking if they wanted to get involved. The response came back like a mighty wind: when do we start?

"We thought we'd buy half a dozen trees and be done," said Toni. "But, boy, did it grow!"

Flight attendants from the DCA base told friends, who in turn told friends from other bases, who told pilots, and soon Toni was besieged with offers of help from hundreds of people across the country, all with suggestions. "They wanted to know how much of the park we could take over."

Toni drove out to Culpeper again, this time to meet with the town council, which was very supportive, as were many of the local businesses. Soon Toni had offers of contributions not only from local architects, but also from nurseries, florists, real estate firms, even a hospital, which offered to donate food for the volunteers when they came to build the garden.

The group chose three days in September, 2002, to start construction. Nearly three hundred volunteers flocked into town to work in three stages: first, the construction crew cleared a large section of the park, while Mitch Hannon, a flight attendant who also owned a construction company, brought his bulldozer. That first day the crew worked with Mitch to produce a grade. The second day another crew, another hundred or so, came in and laid gravel for a trail system. On the third day, another wave of volunteers showed up and planted, using more than three hundred bags of contributed mulch and hundreds of plants, flowers, and trees.

"Irrigation was an issue," said Debbie. "So the volunteers formed a huge bucket brigade. They pulled water from a nearby stream until a generator could be set up to run the irrigation system, which was also contributed. It was incredible."

The volunteers wore shirts with the name KENNIFER MEMORIAL GARDEN, the official name for the project. Chic Burlingame's widow, Sheri, an American Airlines flight attendant, helped shovel, saying the work was a perfect tonic.

"Dirt therapy," Sheri called it.

A week later, a formal ceremony was held to commemorate the garden. A white marble bench provided a focal point in the center of the garden. It was inscribed with a message to Ken and Jennifer: KENNIFER. KEN AND JENNIFER LEWIS, SEPTEMBER 11, 2001. AA/77. The letters etched in the white surface were deep, the words to be seen boldly from a distance.

In addition to the projects for Michelle, Ken, and Jennifer, the DCA flight attendants also contributed to a memorial for Renee May at the Walters Museum in Baltimore. Renee had volunteered at the museum, working to make the building accessible to blind children. As a memorial to her, the DCA volunteers raised money to buy books in Braille.

"It's important to move on, but first you have to feel good," said Toni.

I found that interesting. "What do you mean, feel good?"

"It's always irritated me to hear people say we should get over it. You don't get over 9/11, but you do have to move on. By being part of a project, working with others to create something that had been important to your friends, that gives closure. But it also creates an opening because you leave something positive behind. Something that endures."

Two ideas occurred to me after talking to Toni: first, the notion that closures create openings, which I had not thought of, but the second point awakened for me the notion that working with others could be a useful tool in the struggle to reclaim hope after a tragedy. Part of the process of recovery was getting support.

Dirt therapy, Sheri Burlingame, Chic's widow, had called it. But whatever name the members of the DCA base chose to give their projects, they had discovered a way to harness Anne MacFarlane's connection-making skills to a powerful engine, the power of the group. As a result, I had a fourth clue to recovery from loss: get support.

If you want to get a real boost, find a group of people who all share the same goal.

As Sue Baer said, no one heals alone.

Chapter Twenty-Three
DO WHAT YOU LOVE

W HEN I WAS young a teacher once told me that life offers us many chances to apply our talents. No guarantees on the money, he said, but you'll get memorable people in your life.

I chose aviation for the people. I did it for the skycap with the broad girth at LaGuardia who always had a joke to tell, and for the bus driver at JFK who blew his horn one afternoon as he passed me in front of the Delta terminal. He had been to training that morning, and he gave me a big thumbs up. I did it for the Boston cabbie who popped out of his seat at Logan airport one day in August 2001 to demonstrate how he was now opening doors for people. "I got this much extra in two days," he said as he pulled $47 out of his pocket. It doesn't get any better for a trainer than that.

I did it for the Albanians. Refuges from the civil war raging in their homeland, one Sunday morning forty Albanians approached a man at their church in Boston. Many of them had been doctors, lawyers, and teachers in their home country. Having narrowly escaped with their lives, they were not bashful. They knew the "airport man" worked at Logan, and they asked if he could find them work. But there was a problem. Since they didn't speak English—only one had any English skills—their prospects did not appear bright. Still, the "airport man" had connections, he knew John Duval, and he got them work as dishwashers and bussers in the concession area in Terminal C on the United concourse. Once employed, washing dishes, clearing tables, and mopping floors, the Albanians heard about my "Airport Ambassador" customer service program. They considered it "education," a chance to learn something to give them a leg up in their new country.

"Do they speak English?" I asked John Duval, when John called to ask me if it would be possible to tailor a class for forty Albanians.

"One does," he said. "I think."

"Then we've got ignition," I said. In Miami, where 25,000 cabbies had passed through our "Miami Nice" training, there were days when no one in the class spoke English—yet it had worked. It's all about trying, I believe, and body language goes a long way.

The morning in 2000 when I walked into class with the forty Albanians, I saw a sea of eager faces. It was in their eyes and in the way they leaned forward in their seats. That's when the one who spoke English walked up and introduced himself.

"I'm Michael," he said. "Let me know please if I can help you."

"What were you back in Albania?"

"A teacher," he said. "In the university."

We've got lift-off, I thought, and I positioned Michael at the front of the room next to me. As I went through the lessons, very slowly, including the list of customer service principles, such as smile, look the other person in the eye, speak first—all the basics of good impression-making—I paused after each point. Then I turned to Michael, who turned to the class and translated. What I remember most, a memory that stays with me still, is how expectant, yet blank, all the faces had been while I had been speaking. But the moment Michael spoke, the room erupted into cheers, as the thirty-nine men and women, some in their sixties, pointed fingers at one another, the equivalent, I presumed, of slapping five.

Anne MacFarlane had not used these words precisely to describe it, but when we reach out to others to make connections an electrical charge results. Connection-making is one of life's true wonders, an affirmation of the common humanity we all share, proof that separateness is merely a temporal manifestation.

Thanks to Anne, whose clue had triggered for me the memory of the Albanians, I was learning again about things I had forgotten in the fog of sorrow following 9/11.

I was learning again why I had become a teacher.

Do what you love.

————————

I got some good news when the manager of a mid-sized airport called me to offer training. The airport continued to experience growth, despite the economic upheavals buffeting the aviation industry, but in the process the "hassle-bound" quality of travel had started to wear on his employees. The manager wanted me to offer tips to help his staff deal with the stresses of combining service and security, and I was delighted. After 9/11, security sucked up all training dollars—requiring the cancellation of eighty percent of my contracts—and I saw this as my way back into the game.

Before starting the job, however, I wanted to talk to Sue. Ever since the night, months earlier, when we had sat on her deck at her home, and she said, "Anger doesn't work for me," I had been trying to understand that. How do you do that—get past the anger?

"Turn the page," people said, the advice well-intentioned. But how do we forget the cold, calculating deliberate quality of what they did?

I read a story that men have a harder time with this than women. After a tsunami, for example, psychologists tell us that men find it hard to be idle. The sea takes their fishing boats, and after that they become lost, too. Often these men from villages who have lost the opportunity to work will return to the shore and stand for hours, staring out at the sea—remembering. Women on the other hand, approach recovery differently. Women, the experts tell us, look for ways to make themselves busy. Women delegate tasks. They talk about their emotions and look for things to do, anything to get active again.

"I see the hole still," Jeff Pearse, my mutual friend with Sue had said, and I agreed, which is another reason I wanted to talk to Sue. I had been avoiding Ground Zero. I had not been back in two years, going on three, but one day on a flight from Miami to New York our flight path to LaGuardia took us up the Hudson past lower Manhattan. I had a window seat on the right side, the Manhattan side. It was a clear, blue day—just like that other day.

I thought of a woman, a Port Authority contract administrator, I had worked with on my programs. The morning of 9/11 she had been standing at a window in the North Tower sipping coffee when she saw a plane flying low down the Hudson River. "That's odd," she thought, as the plane flew south. "What is this, some kind of air show?" As the plane drew closer, however, it turned suddenly, coming fast, and it angled directly toward her. She stepped back, falling back, her coffee spilling over her, as American Airlines Flight 11 crashed into the North Tower twenty-five floors above her in a roar of crying steel and glass. How are we supposed to forget an image like that?

As our plane to LaGuardia drew nearer to lower Manhattan I swallowed in anticipation, then I saw it, the gaping hole where the buildings had stood. Tractors scraped along the bottom of the hole, and my heart sank. I counted up in the air to the spot where the 65th floor in the North Tower had been, where I'd had a desk, to the spot I had picked out as I had flown out of Manhattan that morning, and to all the wonderful times I'd had working in the space with my friends. I thought of the coffee cup I had kept behind the photocopying machine, and the receptionist who always had a big hello. But that world was gone now, yet how do we navigate this new, nervous world? Sue would know. She would know how to fish again when you didn't have a boat anymore.

"Hi, Sue, can I talk to you?" I asked after we landed.

"Where are you?" This was becoming our routine.

"At LaGuardia. I was wondering if I could stop over today?"

"Come at three o'clock. By then we should have the lights back on."

Sue once described working at an airport as "managing emergencies," though "thankfully most are not the life-threatening kind," as she had put it. "Just your garden variety annoyances." That day Newark had experienced a garden-variety annoyance, which she had learned the details of when an electric company supervisor had called her at home at 5 AM.

"We got a problem," he said, and Sue gave her normal response: "How bad?"

"The power's gone in all three terminals and on the roadways leading into airport."

With that she had jumped into her clothes and drove in the predawn darkness into the airport. Her senior staff, John Jacoby, Gary Davis, Trevor Liddle and others had gathered to plan strategy. They came up with a plan to turn off all nonessential equipment so that the back-up generators could power the critical areas, such as the jetways and Customs and Immigration computers. The morning rush hour was about to begin and the goal was simple: get the flights out. It worked.

"No delays?" I asked on the phone from LaGuardia.

"The media never called," she said, "which is how I measure our success in cases like this. If anything, people complained that the Port Authority does lousy elevator maintenance, but we're getting electric back. See you this afternoon, three o'clock."

By 3 PM, all the lights had in fact been turned back on. We sat in her office, surrounded by photos of Joe and the kids. The photos included a new addition to her family, "Baby Jack." He was a bright-faced boy with big brown eyes. "My 9/11 baby," she said. After 9/11 Sue had come to see family as more important than anything, and she and Joe had adopted another infant from Guatemala, "Baby Jack."

Sue calls running an airport similar to serving as the mayor of a big city. "The only way to get things done is by persuading people."

She also talks of a "shared vision."

"For this place to operate efficiently, everyone must work together for one goal, to help travelers get through this place safely, swiftly and with people being nice to them."

True to her philosophy, the spaces on the wall between the photos of her family were filled with photos of her staff at Newark, contributors to the "shared vision."

"Flying is all about anxiety," she has said often. "That's why the terrorists used aviation. Put people in tubes thirty-five thousand feet in the air and you make them anxious. That's our job, to make people less anxious. We can only do that if everyone works together."

"What do you draw from to perform at such a high level?" I asked as we sat down at her round table. She likes round tables. Hates square ones.

"I don't think in terms of theories."

"How do you think of what you do?"

"When I began working at the Port Authority in the seventies, I had no female role models. So I decided to operate on my instincts. I do have one principle though, a theory, if you will. I call it my 'mother's theory of management.' "

She credits her mother with having had the greatest influence on her. "My father came from old-line Pennsylvania Dutch," she said. "He was a hard worker. He taught me if you start something finish it, but my mother, she was absolutely indomitable."

I asked her to explain how her "mother's theory of management" applied to running an airport post 9/11.

"Slicing and dicing."

"Slicing and dicing?"

"Focus and do," she said. "As a kid, I remember my dad would announce that we were going to have twenty extra people for dinner. Some new group of cousins had shown up, but my mother never got flustered. She'd just start slicing and dicing."

She leaned back in her seat.

"She'd start right in, my mom, no time wasted. Happens to me all the time, especially at holidays. I'll be about ready to pull my hair out, stuff going on here, plus things I need to do at home, like a holiday party for Joe's staff I had forgotten about. After letting out, 'Aggggghhhh!' I'll get a grip and reach for the cheese and crackers. I'll unpack the crackers and that will give me an idea about what I need to do next. Then I'll do that, the next thing. That will lead me to another thing, and pretty soon I'll have momentum. I'll know exactly how I'm going to get through the rest of the party."

"I read that after a tsumami, the women in a village recover faster than the men," I said. "We men tend to stand on the beach, staring at the sea, remembering."

"You can't do that," she said. "You have do what you can. Clear some brush. Build a tent. Whatever it takes. But I recognize the trouble men can have. After 9/11, one of the police captains told me the car ride home was the hardest part for him. He said he drove fast to make it hurt less."

"What did you do?"

"I used that time differently. Those were the times, in the car, when I would cry. But because I hurt after 9/11, did that mean I could stop pressing ahead? No way. That would have been unfathomable. Mothers teach us how to take care of people. It wasn't about me, this tragedy. I couldn't think of myself. I had to help others."

"How?"

"Help them get moving again. People need to take the first step, do that on their own, but if I can support them, then I'm doing my job."

"Nobody heals alone?"

"Right."

There it was, an expansion of the principle I had learned from Anne MacFarlane, to make connections. Do that, reach out, take the first step, and progress will result. But how do you do that, take the first step? I asked Sue what she was most proud of after 9/11.

"That they couldn't beat us. They threw all this at us and we did not capitulate. I did have one problem though—with Nicky. A mother's problem."

She sat back again, took a deep breath.

"A week before 9/11, I had taken Nicky and Elizabeth into the Trade Center to see everyone. Elizabeth was in a stroller, but Nicky, being himself, scampered off to all corners of the 65th floor. I found him in Bill DeCota's office. He was standing with Bill at the window, as Bill pointed down at all the cars and buildings and ships.

"After 9/11, I didn't let Nicky see the television, because of the replays of the buildings burning, but you can't keep things from kids. He would go to his friends' houses and I noticed he was very silent when he came home. 'What's the matter, honey?' I asked, and he said, 'Is your boss all right?' I told him not to worry, that Bill was fine. 'Nothing happened to Bill.' I said. But I could see he was troubled. So I called Bill and he talked to Nicky on the phone for a long time. After that Nicky's face brightened and he ran outside to play with the super-soaker."

"People don't realize how deep the effects of 9/11 go."

"For women especially. For women, the stakes are enormous. Those who did this, the radical Islamic fringe, want to take women back to the Stone Age. They want to take us back to a time when women's brains weren't considered worth developing, when women could have their hands cut off for minor offenses, or be sexually mutilated by law. That's why this struggle is so critical, and that's what I had to come to ultimately, the conclusion I had to make, that evil exists in the world, and that it needed to be eradicated. That was very hard for me, with my generally liberal attitude."

Ah, there it was! Something had not come easy to her. I wanted to know more. How do we admit to the evil in the world, yet avoid becoming so angry that it stops us? How do we take the all-important "first step," when our outrage is not only great, but justified.

"Yes?" she said, but the question wasn't directed at me. It was directed at Rosa, her secretary, who stood in the doorway.

"Police need you."

"What's up?"

"Another plane with a suspected case of SARS."

"Where from?"

"Seoul."

"Where is it now?"

"On the taxiway. They're holding it, to quarantine the passengers."

"Media call yet?"

"Not yet."

"Good." She turned to me, but I was already standing. "Gotta go. We'll finish another time."

"Of course, " I said. I had my question, the one I had come to ask, but it would have to wait. There were two hundred-plus people sitting on a taxiway who had been up in the air for fourteen hours. Now Sue, their "Mayor" of sorts, was about to try to save them another fourteen on the ground.

Another garden-variety emergency—a pair of bookends framing her day.

BOOK *Four*

WHY WE FLY

Chapter Twenty-Four
THE "SPACE"

In his book, *Man's Search for Meaning*, Viktor Frankl, who won the Nobel Peace Prize, identifies a "space" that exists between stimulus and response. Some call this space "free will," the idea that we can create a separation between cause and effect, but what Frankl is describing really is our ability to choose a response for anything the world might send us. He calls it a "space," the same thing Janet Ott calls our "filter."

Frankl used a personal story to illustrate his point about taking control of circumstances. During World War II, he was imprisoned in a Nazi concentration camp where each day his captors would give him a bowl of dirty water and a rancid fish head as his daily meal. Rather than be appalled, a response his captors intended as their means for reducing him, Frankl did the opposite: he chose to find beauty in the fish head. Why? Because he wanted to tell his story, and to do that he needed to survive. Frankl had found a purpose. His purpose, to survive to tell his story, gave him the energy he needed to withstand any adversity. Frankl had discovered his "one thing," something he could use to resist external pressures. We do not need to give ourselves over to the control of others, or to events, he proved by his example. We can control our destiny if we to use the "space" between stimulus and response to choose an action to move "forward."

One day I got a call from Janet Ott, out of the blue. She wanted to know if I'd be willing to assist at one of her workshops. Someone had taken ill, she said, and she asked if I'd be willing to fill in.

I had not seen Janet in several years, not since shortly after 9/11 when we shared a cup of coffee in a local café. I had told her that day about flying over the twin towers moments before the first plane had struck and how I had been unable to get that image out of my mind. Was it a coincidence that she would call now, days after I had returned from my rejection at the mid-sized airport and just when I needed a lift? Maybe, but it didn't matter, because now that I was seeing the world as Kathryn did (no coincidences) and taking my cue from Anne MacFarlane's philosophy around making connections, and committed to always say yes.

So I said yes to Janet, and it changed my life.

During her session, Janet talked about Victor Frankl and his concept of a "space" between stimulus and response. As Janet teaches it, the world sends us data, whether a rainy day or nineteen brutal men on airplanes—all of which is beyond our control—but we do not need to succumb to events. We can control what we do with the "data."

Our "filters" work as follows to determine how we process events: when things occur in the world, we run the "data" through our personal set of core beliefs, including our opinions and assumptions about the world, to come to "judgments." These judgments give us the "story" we tell ourselves. Convinced about the "rightness" of our personal "stories," we make choices—and in turn, these choices give us our results. But as Janet says—"If you don't like the results you're getting in life, don't look to the end of the process. Go to the beginning. Get curious about the core beliefs you hold that inform your choices as you "filter". Then use the "space" between stimulus and response to make choices that work for you."

The recovery ideas—core beliefs—I had received to this point, soldier on (from Sue,) take time (from Kathryn,) make connections (from Anne), and get support (from Toni,) provided a base for Janet's lessons, including her point about the Law of Attraction; namely, that we get what we pay attention to.

"Change your core beliefs, and you will focus on things differently," Janet said in her workshop that day. "You'll use Frankl's concept of the 'space' wisely and make different choices. You'll get different results—most likely, better ones."

Following Janet's workshop, I got an opportunity to apply her "filtering" lesson. As I came down the escalator at Boston's Logan airport late one afternoon, I looked to the left, toward the Massport Information Booth in Terminal B, and there I saw Anne MacFarlane. She was leaning over a map, pointing out sites for a group of tourists. I had not seen Anne since the day months earlier when we had shared coffee in the Massport break room, but I had been thinking about her. As my plane pulled to the gate that day in Boston, I wondered if she might be working. Then I turned the corner, and there she was— voila! The Law of Attraction at work.

"Welcome to Boston," she said, as I stepped up to her booth after the tourists had departed.

"Hugs and cups of coffee," I said, and she blinked once or twice before she recognized me and smiled.

"How are you doing, Anne?"

"Fine," she said.

I stepped back to allow travelers with real questions a chance to edge in and ask directions. For five or ten minutes I watched as a continuous stream of travelers approached her counter, and my estimate of Anne, already high, jumped. I watched her field questions about the bus to Framingham, the airlines ("How do I get to Delta?") and the staple, the most often asked question at an airport: "Where's the bathroom?"

Anne greeted everyone warmly as she offered the same greeting she had to me, "Welcome to Boston." She wore her pendant, the one with the photo of curly-haired Marianne, which I assumed she never took off. I was overwhelmed by the way she continued to extend herself, even when people were surly. One man wanted to get to the other side of the terminal, to the USAir side. When Anne pointed to the path through the parking garage, an option that would have taken him a minute, he said sharply, "I don't *do* parking garages."

"Oh?" she replied politely, avoiding the bait, and pointed to the bus stop.

Nary one of the travelers who approached Anne knew what she had been through, or what the pendant she wore represented. Who could have known? Yet she received each person with a smile, showing no bitterness for her burden.

"How are you able to do this?" I asked.

I was still grappling, trying to process my emotions around the deliberate quality of the cruelty that day, but there was something about Anne, the strength she projected, that gave me pause and prompted me to "come out" of myself.

This was the first time on my journey that I became conscious of the various choices I could make (Frankl's idea of a "space" between stimulus and response) and aware of the different paths those choices lead to. Normally, I would have reverted to my currently-held core beliefs, the whole counter-productive litany of them since 9/11, and I would have *heard* Anne's answer to my question, but not *listened* to it. This time, however, I made a conscious choice to consider Janet's point ("If you don't like the results you're getting in life, don't go the end of the process . . .") and I decided to pay attention—truly pay attention—to Anne's answer. This I found ironic, since I had been open to Janet's phone call and attended her workshop only by following a tip from Anne to make connections, but nevertheless, I decided I would not revert to what I believed already. Instead, I would change my beliefs if her answer intrigued me.

Intrigue me, it did! It floored, me. She didn't miss a beat, as she said, "It's what Marianne would expect me to do," and with that my world changed again.

Frankl's notion about using our "space" to control our response to circumstances was no different than what Anne MacFarlane had been doing (making connections,) or what Kathryn (taking time), or Sue (soldiering on), or Toni Knisley (getting support), Debbie Roland, or John Duval, or Terri Rizzuto or Steve Bolognese, or any of the others I had gone back to Newark, Logan, and Dulles to visit with after 9/11 had been doing. They were all making choices to use the "space" between cause and effect to assess core beliefs they carried on their filters and create responses that worked for them. The world sends us a bowl of dirty water and a rancid fish head, as it did for Frankl, or it sends us brutal men on a bright blue day, but the world cannot control how we react to those horrors. The world cannot control us—no one can—since we have the power to choose how we are going to react.

"How are you able to do this?" I had asked Anne as she worked in her booth that day at Logan, meaning face her loss with such courage and grace. It was the question I had been seeking an answer to since I had stood on the porch at the Panther Motel, the question that I had been asking since I found myself "stuck" after 9/11 and wondered where the "tightness" was coming from, the true source of it, and how to gain release from it. Now Anne had provided me with an answer, an answer anyone can use to move forward again after loss, a secret to rediscover hope.

Find a purpose.

She had chosen to focus "out" not "in." She had made a choice to step outside herself for others. She walked back out onto the same floor the men who had taken her daughter had walked, but she was not doing it for herself, to satisfy her own needs. She was doing it for a purpose greater than herself. She was moving forward by doing for others.

She was doing it for Marianne.

Once I saw Anne's core belief in action, I could only marvel at my friends and colleagues and at the core beliefs they held that had allowed them to rise up. What were these core beliefs, assumptions and opinions? Duty, for one. Competence. Hard work. Loyalty. Responsibility. Accountability, most of all.

"Somebody had to do it," was the way Toni Knisley had put it when I asked why she'd taken on so much after 9/11. "It's what people needed," said Debbie, who with Toni had coordinated many of the charitable projects the DCA flight attendants had thrown themselves into.

"It had to be done," John Duval said in Boston, in regards to security enhancements that needed to be put in place after 9/11, enhancements that required him to put in sixteen-hour days, including going into the airport at 2 AM to check perimeter locks on airport gates.

Bernie Schettino had said, "We tried to show them our hearts." And, of course, this from Sue Baer: "We're Ops. That's what we do. We soldier on."

I got a call from Steve Bolognese asking if we could get coffee.

"Where?" I said. "Your office at Logan?"

"No," he said. "I don't have an office anymore."

"You left United!"

"Let's get coffee."

* * *

We met at a Starbuck's in New York. After United filed for bankruptcy, Steve learned that his position had been eliminated.

It wasn't the company's fault; the economics in the airline industry had been undergoing a major paradigm shift prior to 9/11. The events of 9/11 only exacerbated and execrated the problem.

I couldn't help but consider the irony: on September 10, 2001, when Steve had called me with the news that we would be working together to create a national program for United Airlines, he had been on top of the world. That had been an important goal of his, to manage a program that would touch everyone in his company. Now it was gone, the chance to build a dynamic customer service program, at which he had worked so hard. "From the top of the world to the bottom in twenty-four hours," he said. What would he do, I wondered? We shared a bond around that phone call he made to me at 6 PM on September 10.

He had landed some consulting work since leaving United, but what truly floored me was his announcement that he had started law school.

"Law school!"

"The thought of taking on a challenge like that was too daunting for me before 9/11," he said.

"I would have rationalized many reasons to myself, including it was too big of a mountain to tackle. Doing something so bold, stepping outside my comfort zone would have been a mountain blocking me. Back then I never believed that I could take a step as big as applying to law school."

There was that term, "too big." Such a debilitating negative power in those two words.

"What made you go for it?" I asked.

"After what we went through at the station, it tested me beyond my limits. In retrospect, 9/11 taught me that life is not a dress rehearsal—something I knew in theory—and that suddenly, mountains were not mountains anymore. What we thought of as problems, issues, and insurmountable obstacles—things like labor issues or scheduling, became much less so. I became more determined not to let this beat me. The airline industry is highly regulated. There are procedures and protocols for much of what aviation does. But there was no "playbook" in the aftermath of 9/11. There were no signposts telling us how to recover. But somehow we did. The entire industry pulled together in an unprecedented way. The mountains become small hills, I knew I needed to set out to take on life in a bold new way, and to turn the negative energy surrounding 9/11 into a positive motivating force that would challenge me further."

"How did you do in your last tests?"

"Pretty good."

Later, I was to learn from Mark Hussey that Steve had placed fourth in his class.

We slapped five, turning a few heads in the coffee shop as we made a nice loud smack with our palms. Hey, I was proud of my guy!

———————

I had set out looking for an answer to the unanswerable question—how do we forgive the unforgivable—some explanation that would unlock the mystery of recovery, but there is no mystery, I realized after talking to Steve. Recovery from loss is quite simple actually: we need to find a purpose then make a choice to "do." We need to put aside our core beliefs about mountains blocking us and instead see problems as obstacles to overcome—challenges to meet.

Later, in a phone call, I asked Steve what he was going to do with his law degree.

"Get back in the game," he said. "On a new level."

I had seen it with Anne, and now I was seeing it with Steve—he wanted to contribute, be a player. He was making a commitment to move forward again. He was determined to get back in the game.

Who needs a fishing boat when you've decided to fish again—on a new level?

Chapter Twenty-Five
CAPTAIN OBVIOUS

J UST WHEN I thought I was finding my way, I got some bad news. The manager who had hired me at the mid-sized airport to develop a training program for his stressed-out staff got fired. He tangled with city commissioners over an airport expansion program, and they fired him. Here one moment, gone the next! But his going meant I was a goner too, because a week later the man the commissioners had appointed to replace my guy called me into the office.

"We're going in a different direction," he said, and I understood what he was telling me. He wanted to put distance between himself and his predecessor, who had sparkled. Happens all the time in business, a triumph of ego, especially when the new guy's so gray people call him, "What's-his-name."

"We're going to take the training program in house," he said. "You can understand our position." I didn't need to hear more.

"Right," I said, as I thought to myself, using a word favored by my guys at JFK: "*Fock!*" But the upshot was that I was back in the arms of anger again.

———————

They say hell is fire. Don't believe them. Hell is an economy motel in yet another city far from home where you turn in bed at 3 AM knowing that the guy you've come to meet in the morning to ask for work will say no. It was that kind of world now, security sucked up the dollars.

One day when our daughter was home from college, she asked if I wanted to play a board game.

"I'm busy right now," I said. She paused before walking away, and I could feel I had slighted her, so I followed her. I caught her as she sat down in another room to watch TV. "I have a lot I'm thinking about right now," I said, trying to make right.

"Yeah," she said.

"I do. I've got a lot on my mind."

"I'm not home that often anymore, Dad. It's not like we have that many chances anymore."

"I know, but I don't have time for games."

"You didn't die on a plane with your nervous guy that morning, Dad."

She looked at me, waiting for my response, but I didn't have one. What could I say? I didn't know I had been that transparent. Silence ensued, and after a long awkward moment, I walked away. This time she followed me and caught up to me in the hallway where she faced me, toe to toe.

"Why do you have to hold onto your anger so tightly?"

"I'm not angry."

"Oh, really? Then what are you?"

"I'm mad."

"What's the difference?"

"Mad gives me the control."

"Is that so, Captain Obvious?" Could this be the same girl that had once ridden a Strawberry Shortcake tricycle on Friday evenings to pick up pizza? "You never talk about it. You never share what you're thinking with me or mom. Where's the control in that?"

"Anger gives them the victory they came looking for," I said. "I'll be damned if I'll ever give them that satisfaction."

"Great. Now you can climb into your cocoon of bitterness and never come out."

"I'm doing this for you."

"For me!"

"You made the point about how much 9/11 has affected everyone."

"I didn't ask you to give your life over to it. I didn't ask you to become a ghost."

"When you do something, take something on, you've got to do it right."

"Whichever way you want to put it, Dad, you're still corroding your soul." It's nice to have a philosophy major in the family. Again I walked away, but this time she didn't follow me, only flicked off the light in the hall, leaving me in the dark.

We have a little tavern not far from our house. It has friendly bartenders, Todd and Jeremy. They know all about the Seattle Mariners. That evening I went down to visit them, to discuss the Mariners pitching rotation. No, hell isn't fire. Hell is that suspended state between Mark Hussey's "remembering" and "moving on," and not knowing how to get unsuspended. Give me a bad third starter in the pitching rotation any day. When I came home, the house was quiet. My wife was in bed. All the lights were out.

"Where's Caitlin?"

"She drove back to school."

"At night? In the dark? It's raining again."

"Did you two talk tonight?"

"A little. I've been trying to get an answer to a question for her."

"Which is?"

"It's a big question. It's not easy."

"Your problem is you want life to be easy."

"Not easy. Just not so brutal."

"That's what makes life hard," she said. "You can't not feel again."

Out the window the moon shone in a cloudless sky. Somewhere in the distance a train whistle sounded. I can tell you what's not easy: two people lie in bed—they face the wall in opposite directions, and neither party sleeps.

That's hell.

"My nervous guy," That's the name I had given to the man on my plane that morning, my 8:20 AM flight out of JFK. It was his eyes, the absence of light. All his energy turned inward. The "vacuum" of his eyes.

For four days after our flight was diverted to Toronto, I sat on the bed in my hotel room trying to make sense of the blur that morning had become. The pilot hadn't told us anything after we had turned around to land in Toronto, only that, "We can't continue onto Seattle. The radar is out in the western United States."

I sat staring at the TV, as stunned as everyone else. I watched CNN replay the tape of the attacks, the North Tower burning, followed by a second plane striking the South Tower, then the towers falling, first the South Tower, then the North. The story cut to a fire raging at the Pentagon in Washington, DC and to a smoldering patch of Pennsylvania farmland. On and on it went; the images searing deep into our collective soul.

On the second day after the attacks, CNN ran a story on the ticker across the bottom of the screen that hijackers may have targeted planes out of JFK. The report told of a United Airlines plane that had been called back to the terminal shortly after 9 AM, after Sue Baer had started the chain of Port Authority airport closures. Four Middle Eastern men had jumped out of their seats demanding that the pilot take off, according to the report, but once the plane returned to the gate, the four had disappeared into the crowd. I thought of my "nervous guy" and caught a shuttle to the airport to find a Canadian policeman. Maybe it was nothing, what I had seen on my plane, the

Middle Eastern man bouncing up and down on his toes for ten minutes before departure, then again maybe it was.

An agent at the American Airlines counter called the Royal Canadian police for me and soon a tall, strapping guy appeared. He had broad shoulders and a wide-brimmed hat. I told the cop how after we became airborne, I had faked a trip to the restroom. I had never done that before, I told him. I had flown a million miles in my career, but I had never gotten out of my seat to check out a fellow passenger. Still, the nervous guy's squirming in the aisle had upset the peaceful tranquility of my morning so much that I had wanted to get another look at him once we got airborne.

I saw he was sitting in an empty row four empty rows behind mine, Row 29. As I approached him, however, he looked different. All his squirming had subsided and he sat staring blankly, almost catatonically, out the window. He seemed diminished, smaller, and I thought, my God, he's pouting!

Then he turned to look at me, and we locked eyes at three or four feet. I continued to hold his stare as he glared at me, and my first thought, "Man, those are damn cold eyes. *Soulless* eyes."

Still, I doubted myself, I told the policeman. It wasn't simply my reluctance to prejudge, though that was a large part of it. The guy hadn't done anything to me, right? So what if he had stood in the aisle before departure making it difficult for people to pass. That made him self-consumed, but there were a lot of self-consumed people in the world. He had cold eyes, too cold for that hour of the morning, but again so what? Maybe he was just a nervous guy sour in the morning before having a cup of coffee. I couldn't say, and I didn't want to presume, so instead I kicked myself.

I had predicated my whole career teaching customer service on the principle of "speak first." Do that, I told airport employees in my classes, 30,000 of them since 1986, and you take control of an encounter. But on this morning of all mornings I had broken my cardinal rule. Had I but asked the guy as he had bounced up and down on his toes beside me before departure, "Are you supposed to be in seat C?" I would have had a voice to go with his eyes. Had he failed to answer, or offered an incomprehensible response, I would have known more about his intentions, whether he was nobody, just another edgy guy, or whether he had come that morning to join with others—who did not arrive—to expand the horror of that day.

But I had failed to act. I had been so excited about my prospects with United Airlines, thinking ahead to January and the chance to work with Mark Hussey and Steve Bolognese to create a national program, that I had blown the chance. Now not having any conclusive proof on the guy, only my imagination, I turned my anger inward. The fault was mine. I had broken my cardinal rule.

"Where did he go, once the plane landed?" the policeman asked.

Once we landed in Toronto, a man at the back of the plane had joked, "Ah, probably just another airline screw up." I had turned for a look at the joke teller and saw him standing at his seat in the last row. There was no one between us, only empty space. My nervous guy had gotten off the plane that quickly.

"I don't know," I said. "When I turned around, he was gone."

The cop folded up his notepad and put his pen away. Click went his pen. Clap went his pad. And with that went my clarity about the world.

The next day, after the skies reopened and I was able to get on a plane again, I sat looking out over the Canadian countryside. I touched the window, as I had four days earlier above Manhattan—my final image of the towers gleaming silver in the sun—but that world was gone now. And a hole as broad and wide and empty as the countryside below had opened to take its place, a world with no signposts to guide us.

"You didn't die on a plane with your nervous guy that morning, Dad," my daughter had said. But in a way I had. I had died to all emotions other than anger, and now the question was clear, the challenge apparent, despite having no signposts:

What does this teacher do now?

"You get what you need, if you're open to it," my trainer friend, Janet Ott, says.

On a trip from New York to Orlando shortly after my encounter with my daughter, I found myself standing behind a family with two young girls at the security checkpoint at LaGuardia. The younger of the two girls, a wispy blonde, was blind. I watched her navigate through the checkpoint, using her red-tipped cane, making a game out of it, and that made me pay attention. I watched as she removed her tennis shoes for an inspection by a security agent, smiling all the while, and I became intrigued. Normally, I would have switched my attention to other matters, such as planning a phone call, but now I focused all my attention on this little girl.

What core beliefs did she carry that allowed her to remain so open, despite her handicap? Twenty minutes later as I boarded my plane, I walked down the chock-filled aisle, navigating through the crowd as I counted rows to number 27, when I saw the little girl and her mother already sitting in Row 27. The little girl was in B, and her mother was in C. Her father and older sister sat in seats B and C in the row ahead of them. I looked at my boarding pass, Row 27, Seat A, and once again, I marveled: the Law of Attraction at work! I was going to get a chance to sit beside this girl for two-and-a-half hours. I followed Anne MacFarlane's bidding to connect, and once we got into the air I asked her where she was going.

"To Disney World," she said.

I asked what ride she liked best, and she said, "The jungle one," and of course I asked why.

"For the scary sounds," she said, and suddenly I understood the essence of this little girl with the clear, blue eyes. She could not see with her eyes, but they were full of light, and in them I saw the core belief that informed her action: she had made a choice to focus on what she had and not on what had been taken away.

I watched her extend her hand through the seat in front of her to touch fingertips with her dad, a game that made her giggle, and I thought what a lucky guy I was to have been given an opportunity to sit next to a little girl and see the world anew.

———————

After we landed in Orlando, I made a call to my daughter at her college.

"Hey, how are you doing?" I said, after she picked up on the seventh ring.

"Fine."

I could sense from her tone that she had learned from me—was learning from me—to withdraw when circumstances made her uncomfortable. If there was anything I could want for her in life, it would be to save her that error.

"I'm sorry," I said.

"It's okay." Same flat tone.

"I'm sorry about the board game, that we didn't get a chance to play."

"I bought it to bring home with me. I don't have a lot of money, Dad."

"I'd like to play next time you're home, if that would be all right," I said, adding, "I know I've been a real asshole."

I don't usually swear with my daughter, but it came out as an act of spontaneity. For nearly three years I had been keeping so much inside. Nineteen men had come to drive us inward, and with me they had succeeded. I had fallen into their trap. Worst of all, I hadn't even been aware of it. I thought I had been resisting them, fighting back, yet all the time I had been succumbing to the internal violence they had marked for us all.

"I'm sorry," I said. "I know I've lost a lot of time with you and mom."

"That's okay," she said, and there was a small shift in her tone. It was barely perceptible, but I could hear a change, as she added, "Welcome home, Dad."

Life can be beautiful, once we change our core beliefs.

I called New Leaf, the flower shop my wife loves in our town. I can't remember the last time I sent her flowers.

"What kind do you want?' the New Leaf lady said on the phone.

"The best you've got," I said.

It felt wonderful to be on my way back.

Chapter Twenty-Six
LETTING GO

As the third anniversary of 9/11 approached, I got an E-mail from Debbie Roland inviting me to join members of the DCA base at the Kennifer Memorial Garden in Culpeper, Virginia. They planned to celebrate the lives of Ken and Jennifer Lewis at the garden they had created in the couple's memory and they wanted me to participate with them. It felt good to be included, to be thought of as an honorary member of the DCA group. Again I took my cue from Anne MacFarlane—always say yes.

And I did—but first I had one final issue to deal with.

———

About this time, *Time* magazine ran an article on the debilitating effects of "unforgiveness." In a cover story on the "new science" of mind and body, *Time* said, "Persistent unforgiveness . . . appears to work to the detriment not just of our spiritual well-being, but our physical health as well," adding, "People with strong social networks—of friends, neighbors, and family—tend to be healthier than loners."

"Forgiveness does not require us to forego justice, or make up to people we have every right to despise. Anger has its place in the panoply of human emotions, but it shouldn't become a way of life."

This last part was the part that continued to give me some trouble. If anger has a place in the "panoply of emotions," where do we draw the line? How do we set a limit? If we have every right to de-spise someone who has committed crimes as horrible as 9/11, how do we keep anger from becoming a way of life?

I wanted to talk to Sue, to finish our conversation that had been cut short in her office the day the plane with a suspected SARS case had landed.

How do I stop anger from becoming the way of *my* life?

It was early September, a bright, blue day, as I walked up the steps to the aviation administration building at Newark. This was the restored 1934 structure that had experienced the roof fire three years earlier. It was a warm day, as well as bright blue—much the way it had been on 9/11.

"Hey?" I said, as I came knocking on Sue's door.

"What are you doing here?" she asked. She stood in the doorway to her office, her coat in hand, about to leave. I had called up from downstairs, and she had told the guard to let me up.

"I've got a question. You got a minute?"

"Heading over to the outlet mall in a moment. I've got forty minutes before my next meeting. The kids need shoes."

"School starting again?"

"Yup." She pointed out the door, in the direction of the parking lot.

"Still driving your maroon Impala?"

"The same."

The same Impala she had been driving three years earlier, the morning she had seen smoke on the horizon, the morning that had changed so much.

"I can come another time," I said.

"No, come. Sit in my office. We can talk a minute before I go. What do you need?" She set put her coat on a hook, and we settled down in leather chairs across from each other at her round table—our familiar venue.

"How were you able to avoid the anger?" I asked, and I pointed back over my shoulder, toward Lower Manhattan. Toward the "hole."

"I didn't avoid it."

"No?"

"I still don't." She said it like that, straight out, using the present tense. "I was angry then. I'm angry still."

"But you don't let anger stop you."

"Anger can be justified, but anger doesn't work for me."

"You said that on your porch that night, but how do you avoid it?"

"I don't avoid it. I just don't buy into it. After 9/11, all the talk was about retribution. But retribution doesn't work for me. It doesn't get me from today to tomorrow, so I don't go there. I don't stay there."

Ah, a distinction, the word, "stay." We were getting closer to something. "That's fine," I said, "but how do you get off 'stay'?"

"Sometimes just putting your socks on in the morning is all you can do to take a constructive step. But that's okay if it gets you out of bed. Tomorrow, maybe you'll take the first real step. There is no one-size-fits all when it comes to grieving, so there can't be any timeline. But taking that first real step has to be the goal. If I can be a cheerleader to help you find your motivator, the thing that works for you, then I'm happy."

"Slicing and dicing?"

"Whatever works for you; it's all about what works for *you*."

Once again her mantra: focus and do. Whatever works for you. But I had a question. "Did you ever have doubts?"

"Yes! I still do. I went to all the memorials, all but one."

"Whose did you miss?"

"A mother. I had recently interviewed for a job. We'd had a great chat about our families and careers. She had four kids. That one I couldn't do. I couldn't bring myself to attend that one, not for a mother with four kids. It still haunts me, and pains me, every day, that I didn't go. It gives me doubts about my ability to do what's right."

"How do you get over those doubts?"

"You've got to."

"How?"

"I focus on what I need to do to contribute. I focus on the future."

"But how do you take the first *real* step?"

"You've got to have something—or somebody—to do things for."

Ah, there it was, an echo of Anne MacFarlane's core belief: find a purpose. "Like run an airport?"

"Like get an airport running *again*."

"I should let you go," I said. "You've got to get shoes."

"Right."

"But I have one last question. Why do you do this?"

"You mean this job?"

"Taking this on, all this. Getting an airport to run again. Of all the things you could have done, why did you make aviation your life?"

She stood and pointed out the window to the runway where a giant 747 was speeding down the tarmac. "That," she said, and I got up to stand beside her. We watched a jumbo jet come tearing down the runway, its engines screaming.

"What we're looking at right now," she said. "That can be explained by science. Scientists can tell us about that, the physics of it, the lift and thrust, how it happens. But that . . ." The jet lifted itself into the air, slowly at first, then more forcefully as it angled into the unmarred sky. "Nothing can explain that, how *cool* that is. It's a miracle every day."

"How cool that is?"

"The spectacle of it. That's why I do this, to be a player in the process."

Suddenly I understood. It was all about the spectacle—to be a "player in the process." To be part of a community that comes together each day to make that happen, to contribute, as she called it, to lift a jumbo jet into the blue, blue sky. Whether we are part of the group that takes to the air, such as the flight attendants and pilots, or play a role on the ground, providing support, we are all "players" in the process, "participants in the spectacle." I watched as the plane grew smaller and smaller, becoming a dot in the unblemished sky. I thought of all the planes I had watched out my window after school, reading their logos. Dreaming about the big, bright world out there. Yes it was cool, to play a role to lift a jumbo jet off the ground. Do what you love, as my teacher once said.

"The glory days," I said. "You're bringing them back."

"We all have a part to play."

We walked toward the door, but at that moment the phone rang. "What now?" she asked, as she picked up the receiver. Then she said, "Who? Okay, okay. I'll wait."

"Another garden variety emergency?' I asked as she hung up.

"I'll find out. They're going to call me back in two minutes. Will you be around later?"

"No, I've got a train to Washington this afternoon."

"Washington?" she said, as she held the phone, waiting for it to ring again.

"The DCA flight attendants from American have invited me to a ceremony, at a garden they created for their friends who died on Flight 77."

"I'd like to meet them."

"And they you." It occurred to me that the people I knew so well from the three airports, Newark, Logan, and Dulles, where the four planes had departed from were friends of mine, but they didn't know each other. If the objective in life is to "do," then I needed to do something about that.

"You're taking a train?"

"Don't worry, I'm not giving up on the spectacle."

"We need your departure tax."

"Don't worry, you'll get your money. I'm set to fly out of here after DC." Then I walked over and gave her a hug. We were standing in the building where commercial aviation had begun in America. I thought of that as I walked over to her, and it felt good to initiate the hug—after all she had given me—in the place where the spectacle had been born, the commercial aviation part of it.

"One of the Port Authority police," she said. "I went to give him a hug last week. He said, 'We still doin' that?' I told him we never stopped."

I walked to the door, but then I turned back one last time, "Did you forgive them?"

"The men?" she asked, looking at me across the room.

I nodded. I didn't need to explain.

"Not that word, exactly."

"Then what?"

"I let them go."

"Ah," I said, and I waved good-bye. She waved once also, when her phone rang. That was so like Sue, to keep her finger on the button, waiting for the phone to ring so all she had to do was lift her finger to begin talking—saving time, a model of efficiency.

Here was a woman who operated on "instinct" rather than theories. She had acted on instinct at 9:03 the morning of 9/11. She had watched a second plane sweep across the sky and strike the South Tower, and she had recognized the event for what it was, an attack on our country. Immediately, she had closed her airport, without regard for herself, her career, or what it might cost her if she was wrong with a million dollar call like that.

Her action had set in motion a chain of events that led to the closing of New York's other two airports, JFK and LaGuardia, seventeen minutes before Federal officials in Washington ordered those airports closed. Who knows if Sue Baer saved any lives that morning? We may never know the full story about that day. But I had the answer I had come for.

"I let them go," she had said.

It's what Sue Baer did instead of letting anger stop her.

Unforgiveness. It "appears to work to the detriment not just of our spiritual well-being, but our physical health as well," according to the *Time* magazine article.

I had two enduring images I carried from that morning, an image of the twin towers gleaming silver in the sun, but also the image of a man with eyes that reflected no light. Was he a figment of my imagination, that man with the cold, cold eyes who had sat in Row 29 and had glared at me after I had gotten out of my seat to check him out? It didn't matter, I realized now, as I stepped outside Sue's administration building. In the end it didn't matter if my "nervous guy" was real. What was real was this: a group of men who had allowed their eyes to become "vacuumed" of all compassion, who had deadened their eyes to the common humanity we all share, had boarded four airplanes at the eight o'clock hour that morning. They had carried out monstrous acts, exceeding the pale of civilized behavior. Possibly I had confronted that evil, as Sue called it, at a very close distance. But ultimately, it didn't matter. Only what was real mattered. More than three thousand people had been struck down by those men.

Mark Hussey was right, every moment since 9/11 has been a tug between "remembering" and "moving on." That was the challenge: how do we find a balance between those two choices, enough that we can gain release not to move "on," but to move forward—and there is a difference.

Any time I saw the pictures from that morning, the tape of Flight 175 slicing over Battery Park on approach to the South Tower, all I could think of was Marianne and Jesus: Marianne with her concern for her colleagues working a delayed flight in Boston that summer morning in 2001 when I had met her; Jesus with his big brown eyes pleading with me to let him sit down so he wouldn't have to play a mean customer; And the couple with the baby stroller at the gate that morning. The stroller the United agent in Boston had folded up in the jetway as he had waved good-bye to the dad and reassured the mom that he'd have it waiting for them at the other end.

How do we process that? How do we stop carrying our pictures of that morning? If we give ourselves over to those images of "remembering," awe will get ourselves "stuck." But how could I not think about what might have been: who "my nervous guy" was, and what he might have wanted to do? I wanted to believe the official reports, that only nineteen men had been involved, but I had my own eyes, and my own experience of people, and I couldn't be sure. But that's where I had found myself stuck, in the remembering, thinking that maybe those eyes had belonged to a man who had wanted to put me and the people on my plane into a building with innocent people.

As I turned to glance back up toward Sue's office, I made a decision thanks to four words uttered by this woman who lived life at full tilt, who lived by instinct and taught by example. I realized we do have a "space." We do have the capacity to pause between cause and effect and choose "forward" over "on," and there is a difference. "Forward" breaches the gap. It solves the suspended state. "Forward" admits to emotions and confronts core beliefs that don't work anymore and chooses beliefs that work. "Forward" takes us out of ourselves and produces the progress we seek—it requires that we think not only of our needs, but of the needs of others.

We don't move forward by holding back, holding tight to the anger. Forgiveness is not about the other person, as Kathryn had said. Forgiveness is about us making a choice to be free. And so I made that choice. I let my nervous guy go.

Chapter Twenty-Seven

KENNIFER'S BENCH

I FLEW INTO Dulles the evening of September 10, 2004, arriving on the concourse across from Gate D-26. This was the gate Flight 77 had departed from nearly three years earlier. It was a Friday evening, and traffic on the concourse was light. I had planned to take a train to Washington, but took a plane instead. Life is not a straight line. As I stood alone on the carpet in front of the vacant counter, I thought back to what had happened in this space nearly three years earlier.

Michelle Heidenberger, Renee May, and Ken and Jennifer Lewis had gathered as a group in front of this same gate. Chic Burlingame would have been on the plane already with David Charlesbois, the co-pilot. After Michelle wrapped up her call with Toni Knisley, the flight attendant friends would have hurried down the jetway in advance of general boarding, followed by five men who would introduce a new form of cancer into this country.

Above me, the CNN monitor played against the quiet backdrop. Sports, weather, and a continuous stream of *Headline News* stories poured forth, but I was struck by one story, an interview with a man named, Dr. Ajami, a professor at Johns Hopkins University. A tragedy in Beslam, Russia, had occurred days earlier, an assault on an elementary school by radical Islamic militants. I felt a stab of hopelessness, a sinking sensation as I pondered how the violence that had been initiated, in part, in this space had accelerated. In many ways the world had moved in darker directions since that bright, blue morning, and one could despair that the men who had come to drive Americans into divisive camps had succeeded. Bin Laden, the mastermind of 9/11, wished to turn civilization on itself, roll it back, undo centuries of progress man has achieved through painfully small steps. 9/11—with its searing images broadcast around the world—was intended, in his cynical, brutal mind, to be a recruitment call for a clash of civilizations. How else to view the events in Beslam, as disaffected young men rallied by Bin Laden turned themselves into suicide bombers. It was enough to cause despair, but the professor took a different tact.

"I am hopeful," said Ajami. "I think the tragedy in Russia has sent a signal to moderate Muslims around the world. No longer can Muslims claim that 9/11 was an aberration. They must acknowledge that radical elements are using our religion for violent purposes. I am hopeful, if one can be hopeful, that moderates will move to the fore and exert their influence."

Yes, that was a worthy call; moderates move to the fore! Moderate Muslims needed to take a stand against suicide bombing. We all needed to see the shades of gray in the Muslim world and avoid falling into the trap set for us, a trap the whole goal of which was to precipitate a war between civilizations.

"I am hopeful," Dr. Ajami said, and so was I, ever the optimist, that the light of reason might shine again, that the humanity that binds us all might be affirmed—so that some good might yet come from the horrific events that had their genesis at Gate D-26.

———————

The next morning I drove a rental car out of DC, turning west to the open country, toward Culpeper, Virginia, two hours away. The city gave way to rural in stages, much like peeling off layers of clothes, and I wondered if that is why Ken and Jennifer Lewis had chosen to live out this far. The sign entering Culpeper said, WELCOME TO ONE OF AMERICA'S BEST SMALL TOWNS.

Ken and Jennifer had been adventurers, I'd been told, but what, I wondered, had they been like as people? I knew that Jennifer, thirty-six, had planned to give Ken a new motorcycle for his fiftieth birthday. But there was something about them: a special quality that came through in the tone of their friends' telling and the look in their colleagues' eyes when they spoke of the couple. It was obvious that Ken and Jennifer Lewis were well loved. Long before there had been a Ben Affleck and Brad Pitt and whatever starlets they had become paired with, there was "Kennifer," a name that spoke of the Lewis' not as two, but as one. I was looking forward to learning more about them. What was it about this couple that had inspired their friends to re-make a patch of park into a garden and come back, time and again, to celebrate Ken and Jennifer's lives?

What core beliefs had they lived by that they had earned such affection from so many?

———————

Yowell Park, a broad, sweeping expanse of trees and broad lawns, sits outside the town square of Culpeper. I glanced at the map Debbie Roland had E-mailed and saw that the Kennifer Memorial Garden was at the far end of the park. Debbie's directions advised following the stream. Three hundred American Airlines staff and friends had created the garden, and I was anxious for a glimpse of it, a symbol of life's rejuvenating power.

I turned a corner around the stream and came upon three men with close-cropped hair. They had square shoulders and flat stomachs, pilots, I assumed, and I watched as they built a tent. More people arrived, some carrying coolers, others with boxes. Debbie had told me that this event was intended as a memorial, but after two years of solemn anniversary memorials, members of the DCA base had decided they wanted to have a picnic following the memorial, to celebrate the lives of their friends as well as remember their loss. Debbie arrived, and we exchanged a hug before she turned and introduced me to a group of people, including two Kate's, one who flew out of Chicago and the other Miami—yet they lived in Washington.

"You really do that?" I asked. "Live in Washington, but fly out of other cities?"

"We love the DCA base," they said, simultaneously. "We once belonged to this base, and we didn't want to give up the connections."

I could see why, as I was introduced to more people who offered warm greetings: May, Alex, Valerie, Kim, Carolyn, Nancy, Wendy, Heidi, and more. I didn't get any last names. It was a picnic, as well as a memorial, and informality would prevail.

"Working on this project two years ago, that was the first time I had laughed in a year," Heidi said, and I understood how important it was to these members of the DCA base that they have a picnic as part of their day, to give themselves a chance to laugh, as well as remember. The formal ceremony began shortly after noon. The group, fifty to sixty, drifted up a pebbled path to the center of a space filled with trees and flowering bushes, and to a white marble bench, which provided the focal point. KENNIFER, the letters on the bench read. IN MEMORY OF KEN AND JENNIFER LEWIS. SEPTEMBER 11, 2001. AA/77.

A senior pilot, Keith Wilson, pulled sheets of paper from his back pocket and a hush settled over the crowd. Keith paused to compose himself. "I want to talk about two duties," he said. "First, the duty that our colleagues fulfilled that morning, as they continued to do their duty until they could no longer do it. Secondly, the duty we have to them, our duty to remember our friends and colleagues, to never forget."

A sweet fragrance wafted from the tress and bushes but the air remained still. The stillness was punctured by sniffles. I found it very powerful to think of duty as a dual responsibility. It was clear these men and women from the DCA base were fulfilling their duty to their friends, the duty to remember them, but it was good also to hear Keith talk about the bravery of the flight crews. I was pleased to see

him salute not only the crew from American Flight 77, but also all
the aviation heroes who died that day. He read their names, the crew
from all four planes, one at a time:

"The crew of American Airlines Flight 77: pilots Charles
Burlingame and David Charlebois; flight attendants Michelle Hei-
denberger, Renee May, Ken, and Jennifer Lewis. The crew of Amer-
ican Airlines Flight 11: pilots John Ogonowski and Thomas
McGuinness; flight attendants Barbara Arestegui, Jeffery Collman,
Sara Low, Karen Martin, Kathleen Nicosia, Betty Ong, Jean Roger,
Dianne Snyder, Amy Sweeney. The crew of United Airlines Flight
175: pilots Victor Saracini and Michael Horrocks, flight attendants
Robert Fangman, Amy Jarret, Amy King, Kathryn Laborie, Alfred
Marchant, Michael Tarrou, Alicia Titus. The crew of United Airlines
Flight 93: pilots Jason Dahl and Leroy Homer, flight attendants Lor-
raine Bay, Sandra Bradshaw, Wanda Green, CeeCee Lyles, Deborah
Welsh.

Thirty-three names, heroes all.

Keith folded his pages, crinkling them, and put them into his pocket.
Then a man I had not met stepped up. He nodded to the group, as
he introduced himself.

"My name is Andy Malberg," he said. "I know all of you were
like family to Kenny. I wanted to come today to represent his actual
family. Kenny was my cousin."

Andy told how he and Kenny had spent summers together on
their grandfather's farm in southern Virginia when they were growing up. "Grandpa Dowdy never said a bad word about anyone, and
neither did Kenny. Kenny learned that from Grandpa, and I'm sure
that was part of the reason why so many people loved Kenny."

People nodded, dabbing at their eyes. The rest of the day unfolded with hamburgers and hot dogs and warm stories of Ken and
Jennifer. A tall woman named Mary told one tale: "On September
3, eight days before, we were at LAX. We were having dinner, Ken,

Jennifer, Michelle Heidenberger and I. Michelle got up to go to bed, but Ken and Jennifer wanted to play pool, so we headed out, picking up a few others along the way. We played late into the night, but we had to break up Ken and Jennifer because they were winning every game."

"That was the thing about Ken, his energy," said Miami Kate. "I remember flying to Seattle on a trip with him. He rented a car, and he, Jennifer, and I, and a few others went up to Snoqualmie Pass. Kenny led us on trails and through ravines. I'm a city girl, and I never got so muddy."

"Jennifer was the kind who the minute you met her, she was your friend," said a woman named Brett, who wore a t-shirt that read, WITH WINGS ON EAGLES. The shirt had Ken and Jennifer's names below a picture of an eagle soaring.

Debbie Roland had brought several photo albums, and people gathered about, leafing through pages that showed a hundred photos of the Kennifer Garden construction effort.

"Jen and I were roommates before she met Ken," said Heidi. "Tom Pakes, Kenny's roommate, and I decided to fix them up. It took us a while, but once we did, it was love at first sight."

"Friends called them Kennifer?"

"Yup," she said, "because they were two peas in a pod."

Young kids scampered about, some working the line for extra cokes and hot dogs, others pulling on the arms of moms and dads to play softball. I found myself looking at Andy Malberg, who stood by himself watching the kids have fun. His broad open face and his story of Grandpa Dowdy had intrigued me. I wanted to know more about what he and Kenny had experienced growing up on a farm in southern Virginia, and so I approached him.

"I drive a commuter bus from the Maryland suburbs into DC," Andy said. "The morning of 9/11, as I was driving, I could see the smoke, but I never realized." His voice went soft, then he smiled to think of his cousin. "People loved Kenny. He was so full of life."

"What do you remember most about him?"

"His mom and my dad were from a family of fifteen kids. After Kenny's mom got married, she bought a piece of Grandpa Dowdy's farm and built a house. Kenny, the minute he was born, attached himself to Grandpa. He learned everything he knew from Grandpa Dowdy—how to track a deer, how to find his way through the woods. It wasn't until after 9/11 that I realized how much I admired Kenny for all that he had absorbed from Grandpa Dowdy."

I asked if he and Kenny were close.

"After 9/11, for months afterward I kept a newspaper article about Kenny taped to the dashboard of my bus. That's against company rules, but I did it anyway. Then something happened last week that made me go back and find that article." I waited, allowing him to continue at his own pace. "I saw a TV report. It was about a man who lost his wife at the Pentagon. Every day he goes to her gravesite and brings her flowers. He sits down beside his wife's grave and has a conversation with her. Every summer Kenny and I spent weeks together on Grandpa Dowdy's farm, and I wanted to remember Kenny again the way that man remembers his wife. I wanted to remember us growing up. So I taped the newspaper article back up on my bus."

"Is it still there?" I asked.

"It is. One day this week, a lady stepped inside the door and asked, 'What's that?' And I told her, 'That's so I won't forget.' "

Andy smiled, a broad grin that suffused his face. I could see he was thinking about Kenny, about being a kid again and spending time on a farm long ago.

"What do you remember most about that time, back then?"

"Kenny loved to imitate Grandpa. James Dowdy was just a poor dirt farmer. He wasn't nothing to the world. But every time Grandpa walked into town, Kenny on one side, me on the other, all the men in town would stand up and say, 'Hey, there, James Dowdy.' He was so gentle and so open that nobody had a cross thing to say about him. That's what Kenny learned watching Grandpa. He watched him close, and he learned well, that if you respect people and never say anything bad about anybody, you get that back."

I looked around at the memorial garden, at the dozens of people, and I understood what Andy meant. He was offering a wonderful lesson about Grandpa Dowdy and Kenny, which extended to the Law of Attraction. It is important to give back, but I realized that was something Kenny had always known, because he had learned it early.

As I looked out at all the people who had come to this place on this day, many of whom had traveled from far corners of the country, I understood why they loved their fallen colleagues so much. Ken Lewis had learned when he was knee-high, and had never quit learning, that the secret to having friends is to make friends. Whether it's late at night in Los Angeles when you gather a group and go out looking for a pool hall, or you land in a new city and usher people into your car and head to the mountains to teach them to hike, or simply keep an open face and a ready smile, that's a way of life. Do that and when you're gone people will clear a patch of ground and build you a garden. Kenny had learned that lesson watching an old man walk into town with an open face. He learned that we get back what we give to others.

The picnic wound down. Food was repacked, chairs were folded up and photo albums were returned to their sleeves. I walked down the gravel path to the center of the garden and sat on the "Kennifer" bench.

T.S. Eliot wrote: "There is no end to our exploring. We continue to search until we get to the place where we started and see it new for the first time."

I took a deep breath, an effort to extend the moment, as I pondered the deeper meanings of the Kennifer Garden and my year-long (plus) journey to get to this place. I thought of all the lessons I had learned along the way—the clues to recovery I had been given by friends—and I realized the moment marked a milestone. This was important, this moment. It was a big deal.

As I sat on the bench in the quiet of that garden, I felt the coolness of the marble under me, marble that was the product of a tragedy, yet a tragedy that had been tempered by the tremendous power of love. The love was one that had created this bench in response to powerful loss and inestimable cruelty. It was love that had produced a garden in response to brutality, a symbol of the rejuvenating power of life.

At that moment, I knew I had come to the end of my journey, because with that coolness of the bench, that sensation of the marble against my skin, I realized this was the first time in three years that I had *felt*.

Chapter Twenty-Eight

RECLAIMINGTHESKY.COM

F AST FORWARD almost two years, and truly it was fast forwarding because I made a decision sitting on the Kennifer bench that day in 2004, one that marked a new beginning for me. After that, life picked up speed. Early in 2006, I had the opportunity to meet Brad Burlingame, Chic's brother. He sent me a note telling me he was going to be in my town for a business meeting and asked if we could get together for coffee. Always say yes was my new mantra, but this opportunity to meet Brad came because of the decision I had made on the Kennifer bench.

"I'm rarely in this part of the northwest, " Brad said, as we sat at a window table in a local coffee house. "What a coincidence."

"I used to think so," I said. "That there were coincidences."

"Me too," he said, and I sensed a bond with him immediately. "But no longer. Now I understand that everything happens for a purpose."

He told me how for two years after 9/11 he had stopped flying American Airlines. Brad was the brother Chic Burlingame had been flying to L.A. to see to celebrate his birthday on September 11, 2001. They had planned to attend an Angel's baseball game together, their mutual passion. Brad looks strikingly like Chic, and after 9/11 he said he found it too painful to fly American, since flight attendants wanted to talk to him.

"Flight attendants would stare at me as I sat in my seat at boarding time. They looked at me as if they knew me," he said. "After we'd get in the air, they'd check the manifest and find my name, 'Burlingame,' and they'd tell me how sorry they were. It got to be too much to bear, and for two years I stopped flying American."

Brad is the president of a convention and visitors bureau in southern California and flies a lot.

"But then I made a decision," he said. "I made a decision to embrace my loss, and it has made all the difference."

Now he flies American Airlines as often as he can, and every chance he gets he tells the crew how much he appreciates all they are doing in the face of adversity.

That day as I had sat on the bench, the sun setting behind me, I realized why I had gone back to the people I did, and Brad's point about "embracing" his loss underscored it. I went back to the people I did because I had perceived them as strong.

Take Mark Hussey in Boston. He had his staff's three circles of pain to comfort, yet he also had a station to run, and he did it, despite adversity and a lousy aviation economy. Or John Duval and Ed Freni. Someone had failed to perform a security check on a group of bags at an airline gate at Logan in 2002, causing a security breach that could have shut down the airport. This was during a period shortly after 9/11 when nerves were on edge, and so to avert re-screening of all luggage on the concourse, John and Ed—the two top-ranking operations officials at Logan—volunteered to climb in the hold of the airplane to recheck the baggage themselves. In their suits they climbed into the underbelly of an aircraft with flashlights so the airport would not have to be shut down. As a result, thousands of Logan passengers were able to continue on their way, totally unaware that two guys had just saved them hours of inconvenience. That's what had drawn me to the people I chose to interview. It was this quality of quiet heroism, a willingness to come outside of themselves because it was the right thing to do. In the beginning, however, I had believed I could assume the lesson of loss from them; that I could gain awareness of what I needed to know by reflecting in their strength.

But I came up against a cold hard fact. It doesn't work that way. As a boy, I had imagined the world a certain way, with my binoculars trained at the sky. I had read airplane logos and anticipated the big, exciting world out there. But it's also a dangerous world, as Sue says—one where evil exists.

Mine had been an ideal image of the world, one in which I had believed there were lines people did not cross. That was the "too big" quality of 9/11. Steve Bolognese had put his finger on it. The hard part was the deliberate act one group of men did to so many others. But Steve had dealt with it. He had learned from it, and he had learned that the brutality could not break him. Then he took that knowledge and put it into action to move forward again. That was the key. It wasn't enough to know the lesson; we needed to act on it.

After my daughter had nailed me with the "you didn't die that day" line, my wife had told me, correctly, that I wanted the world to be easy. No, I had said, I just don't want it to be brutal. But it *is!* Or can be, and that's the point. We can't avoid the 9/11s, or other horrible things that happen simply because they violate our ideal of how we think the world should be. This teacher needed to become a student to learn that. The world is brutal, but it is also beautiful. It is a mix of beauty and brutality, and that's the challenge in living. Each day we must face that duality of life. But we do not have to allow ourselves to be controlled by the brutal side. We can take control of our lives once we realize that we possess a "space," and we can use our space, our free will, to make a choice to respond with actions that work for us, to move us forward.

But we need to act to achieve that kind of progress.

And that's what I decided on the Kennifer bench: I decided to take an action to move forward and I created a Web site, www.reclaimingthesky.com. The Web site offers people a forum to share ideas around the healing process, to discuss how they are learning from loss, both as an aid for themselves, and as an inspiration for others. But more on that in a moment.

So, yes, gaining release from the suspended state between "remembering" and "moving on," finding a way to move forward, comes down to finding a purpose: find something that works for you. And that's what reclaimingthesky.com has been for me, a chance to communicate, to learn from others on an on-going basis.

Brad Burlingame was among the first to respond to the Web site. He sent me an E-mail, and we got together. Now I have an important new connection: the product of a decision made on a bench and an action taken.

There are no coincidences.

———————

The trail of education that led me to understand all this had began in Sue's backyard on a summer night in 2003 when Sue proffered insight into the first step in the recovery process, to soldier on.

At its most basic level soldiering on means working even when our sadness is so deep no tears will come. But that's when we need to press ahead with the greatest resolve. Get up in the morning, put socks on and take that first step. Clear brush, build a tent, "whatever it takes," as Sue so aptly put it. This was a core belief I learned on my journey: to soldier on, as I had learned another useful clue from Kathryn, to slow down, take time.

We miss a lot in life if we don't take time. I thought of Andy Malberg's story about the man from the Pentagon who visited his wife's grave every day. He brought her flowers and then sat down to have a conversation with her. I could only guess at the pain he felt in missing her, but it's so easy to forget the truly important moments in life. How many games with my daughter had I missed? As I had sat on the Kennifer bench that day, nearly two years earlier, the crackling ripple of the stream creasing the still air, I realized that the "gift" of slowing down was an opportunity for a fresh start. We need to slow down, take time, pay attention—or we lose the chance. The little moments come and go, disappearing as quickly as the leaves on the trees in the "Kennifer" garden, and we never get the opportunity again. Ask the man who brings flowers to his wife's grave.

And a third clue. Sitting on the bench that day, I had begun to absorb, truly absorb, Anne's point about the importance of making connections: remain open to others, let people into our lives. That provides the platform for moving forward. Making connections, by its nature, energizes us to adopt the positive outlook necessary to focus outward. It prepares us for taking the first step to reclaim our lives after loss.

This idea tied in with a fourth clue, this one offered by the DCA flight attendants led by Debbie, Toni, and so many of their flight attendant colleagues. It was beyond me to know their sorrow, to know what it had been like to lose colleagues they had worked with intimately, friends they had sat on a jump seat with one moment, only to have them gone the next. They had taken me in, though, the members of the DCA base, and I had learned something critical from them. Beginning with Kathryn who introduced me to the group, I had watched them make commitments, individually and as a team, to focus outside their own pain. They resolved to move forward by doing for others, and thus had generated a self-perpetuating support system around the ideal of service.

"Create closures that produce openings," Toni had said. That had become the goal of this group—their collected purpose. The charity projects the DCA base chose to initiate, one after another, produced the kind of momentum that helped everyone move forward. No one heals alone, as Sue had said, and DCA flight attendants proved that by their actions, inspiring me in the process.

And finally a fifth clue. I thought of Ken Lewis and the picture his cousin Andy had painted of him as a small boy walking beside his grandfather in rural southern Virginia. Kenny had watched Grandpa

Dowdy walk into town, smiling as he came, and as such he had learned how to become open and accessible. This had led Kenny to be open and accessible in his own life, and with his wife and partner, Jennifer, they had applied their openness at every opportunity. Yes, they were "too good," too good for the fate that befell them. But as I sat on the bench their friends had created for them, I realized that Ken and Jennifer were offering a new idea—to engage.

Live life as a full participant. Live fully engaged. Savor moments. Savor them again and again. That is how we get to the marrow of life. That is how we make the best use of our time in the short time we are given. Time runs out too soon, often ending inexplicably, but we miss mightily if we fail to adhere to these clues I'd been offered.

Soldier on.

Slow down, take time.

Make connections.

Seek support.

And this latest core belief from the Lewis', to live fully engaged.

As I had sat on the bench that afternoon, running my fingers over the letters engraved in marble, "Kennifer," I thought of all the people I had met on my journey, friends I had known, but new sides of whom I had gotten to see. I thought of their strength, which led me to think of the meaning of the word "strong." What I realized is that strength lies in our ability to do whatever it takes to move forward.

I had hated the word, "forgiveness." I had fought hard against it, but I realized, sitting on that bench, that forgiveness is the strongest word in the language because forgiveness—letting go—is the only word that meets the requirement for healing. It is the only word that moves us forward, beyond the clutches of those who came to turn us inward, to make us fearful of each other and reluctant to connect.

It's the only word that sets us free.

All these clues were something that could not be grasped with the head. These were lessons that could be understood only through the heart:

First: soldier on, take time, make connections, get support, and live fully engaged.

But that must be combined with "letting go." As Kathryn said, "Forgiveness is never about the other person. Forgiveness is a choice we make."

Finally, the third part of learning from loss: find a "purpose." Use the positive energy that comes from the two previous steps to look beyond our own needs and to the needs of others. The people I went back to in Boston, New York and Washington to explore this issue with didn't know each other for the most part, but the result was the same. Those who were getting "better" were those who had found a way to come outside themselves and do for others.

One more thing, on this point about lessons learned, and it goes to why we fly. Sue put her finger on it: people who work in aviation do it to be part of the spectacle. They do it to be a participant in a community that comes together each day to put planes in the air so others can get where they are going.

They do it so others can keep moving, so the country can keep flying, and growing.

———

Now back to reclaimingthesky.com, and the decision I made sitting on the Kennifer bench.

It involves this book, which we have set up as a platform to apply the lessons revealed here. We've taken the first step, we've created the Web site and a not-for-profit organization around it, and we are looking for projects we can get involved with—projects that "bring closures that produce openings." All profits from sales of this book, any royalties I might get, will go to support that effort. My role as an author is over. Now I'm one member of a group committed to the goal of making our nonprofit a significant vehicle to support those who keep America flying.

Will the Web site work? By time you read these pages you can check it out. Go to www.reclaimingthesky.com and if there's a charity project announced there, it means we're still going. We'd love it if you considered joining in.

Will it last? Who knows? What I do know, what I realized sitting on the Kennifer bench, feeling again, knowing the joy that springs from the rediscovery of hope, the lightness that comes from believing in the possibility of life again and life's rejuvenating power, is this: we've got to try. Savor the little moments. Become a saver of moments, and take joy in the people we share our time with.

That's how we reclaim the sky.

Epilogue

JANET OTT, my trainer friend, asks, "What would you do if you knew you couldn't fail?" It's great food for thought, and here's how people I met on my journey are faring in that regard, starting with those in Washington, DC.:

In February, 2006, Debbie Roland was awarded a significant safety award, the José Chui Award, for her work as part of an air safety team. The award is the highest safety honor bestowed by the Association of Professional Flight Attendants (APFA), the flight attendants' union. For more than twenty years, Debbie has been involved in in-flight safety programs, as well as serving on accident investigation teams. Or as one APFA official said, "We put Debbie out there, and when we reel her back in, she's got a hundred strangers working together."

Debbie still flies for American, flying the skies between Dulles and L.A.—the same route as Flight 77—but as she said, "Someday I won't be working for American. How can I take all that I've learned, the safety part, as well as the 9/11 part, and move to a new level?"

She went to a career counselor, who helped her identify several passions in her life, including helping others, teaching and communicating. "The thing I learned from 9/11, the greatest lesson from the hard road back, is how important it is to stay open," she said. "From all the projects we did, Michelle's video library, the Kennifer Garden, what I learned is that you've got to put energy out there and trust the universe will give you back the right answer. Before 9/11 I didn't trust that, now I do."

Debbie continues to work hard on packed flights as she takes a personal inventory. Despite the challenges of flying in a turbulent time, including dealing with "air rage" again ("Some days I think passengers forget there was a 9/11,") she remains open, trusting that she will find the next right thing to do.

Toni Knisley has found her "opening" after "closure" in her grandchildren. For three years Toni provided personal support to families of the flight services crew lost on Flight 77 before she retired as the flight services supervisor for American Airlines at Reagan National airport in October, 2004. Now she dotes on her four grandchildren, and now they get it from grandma, "Oh, come on!" when their requests, like staying up late, exceed limits.

Kathryn Ajello also continues to fly the Washington/Dulles to LA route. She remains committed as ever to her garden, and to "life's rejuvenating power." Committed spiritually also, she signs her messages, "Blessings." I found a ceramic tile with that message and sent it to her, and she hung it on the tree in the garden beside her swing, the swing where she had been sitting on the morning of 9/11.

In Boston, there is, and I suppose there will always be, a sense of obligation around safety, or as Ed Freni said to me in his office in September, 2005, "We'll always be aware that they came through *our* airport." Tom Kinton, Massport's aviation director, continues to hold his 8:30 AM security briefing every morning, seven days a week—attendance mandatory. In March, 2006, *USA Today* ran a story lauding Logan for the intensity of its focus on security. "They walked on our floors," Ed said to me one day recently. "Never again."

Ed recently bought a house in Maine, his dream house. It's an unstained, shingle house that overlooks the sea. His eyes light up when he talks about "having a cup of coffee on my deck on a summer morning watching an eagle turn over the unrippled water." It's fitting that Ed, "Mr. Whadya Need?," should get something back.

I feel the same about John Duval. He's getting something back, too. In the spring of 2006, he was chosen by the American Association of Airport Executives to be in line to become president of that national aviation organization in 2009, a huge honor.

Anne MacFarlane retired from Massport in 2004. She stays in close touch with Virginia Buckingham, who was Massport's executive director on 9/11. They share a unique bond, the former head of the agency and the mother who worked in an airport information booth.

Mark Hussey at United is building a cabin in the Maine woods and goes up to frame the cabin with his teenage son. They bond that way, he and the boy, nearly a man now, who wanted him to take the job driving a Coke truck for the hats and free six packs of Classic. Mark plans to retire to that cabin someday.

Steve Bolognese continues to rack up top grades in law school. "The little, low cost carriers, they're not so little anymore," he said. "Maybe they need a lawyer who knows something about customer service." Always eager, always looking ahead, Steve's looking to a new career that combines his twin passions, law and service. Joan Twing continues working part time to have time for her family and grandson.

At United in Newark, Mike Spagnuolo moved over from JFK to replace Terri Rizzuto before going on to become United's station manager at Hartford, Connecticut. There are rumors that Terri, after two years in her family's business, might come back to aviation, but those are more a product of people wanting her to come back. "I'm happy," she told me. "I've moved on. I'm in health care. I'm happy. I'm still helping people."

Eileen Ammiano moved on to hospitality. She works in the sales department of a Newark area hotel, but with Judee Beyer, the vice-president of CAUSE, the charity that assists United Airlines flight attendants in distress, she gives as much time as she can to charity fundraisers for her former colleagues.

Also at Newark, the last time I saw Sue, she was dealing with snow. "We had it all planned," she said to a large group at a post snow storm meeting in February, 2006. "But the snow didn't cooperate. Instead of coming down at the rate of an inch an hour as forecast, it came down at four inches an hour. For the first time in two years we had to close the airport, but we'll be ready next time. We don't want to have to close the airport again, no matter how much Mother Nature throws at us." She remains undaunted as ever by the "garden variety" emergencies.

Bernie Schettino retired from the Port Authority in February, 2006, after thirty-one years, though he continues to call his friends at work. At his retirement party they showed a video of Bernie in sweats running around like Rocky—up sand piles used for snowstorms, through the terminals and (as the Rocky theme played) up the steps at the Administration building. There he turned for his close up with a sign that read, "I went the distance."

Asked what he learned most from 9/11, Bernie, who created the Family Assistance Center for Port Authority victims' families, quoted Gandhi. "The best way to find yourself is to lose yourself in service to others."

Tom Innace, the Port Authority police officer is still on the job and now also runs marathons to keep "moving forward." Other members of the Port Authority administrative team have moved up to new jobs. Gary Davis is head of operations, Huntleigh Lawrence is the chief of landside operations and Trevor Liddle works with the airport redevelopment team. Frank Loprano is still the chief of airside operations, reporting to John Jacoby, the airport's deputy general manager.

John had an interesting observation on what he's learned since 9/11.

"At this airport, we've always had a sense that team is important," he said. "That comes from Sue, but since 9/11 we feel that more strongly, and I think we act on it consciously. We keep an eye out to see how people are responding emotionally. That's the role of a manager, and Sue promotes it, to monitor the organization's people and get them help if they need it."

He told of a friend, a colleague he had met through his Peace Corps contacts in the 1970s, when he had worked in the mountains of southeast Asia. "My friend was supposed to leave Sri Lanka on Christmas Day in 2004, but his plane was delayed," John said. "As a result he was there when the tsunami hit. He saw first-hand the destruction, and since that time has dedicated himself to studying trauma, including the effects of post-traumatic stress on people.

"In the third world, traditionally, they don't give a lot of attention to the "After," but I think there's a lesson for us here in the United States. Nine-eleven didn't just happen to people in New York, Boston, and Washington. It happened to all Americans, and the effects are more far reaching than I think people are ready to admit. We need to pay more attention to the under the radar effects of trauma, which can manifest in various negative ways, and linger long after an event. In a very real sense, the time long after a disaster is as critical as the time *immediately* after it."

John's comments struck a chord with me, because that's the direction I found myself heading also. I stopped Sue after her snow meeting to ask her for a final word on the lessons we might take from the tragedy of 9/11—how would she suggest we learn to live with hope in an era of ever-present anxiety?

I caught her on the run, of course, but she pointed toward her office and the round table where she offered me a few minutes before the calls started pouring in that would dictate the direction of her day.

"We must move forward," she said. "Life calls us forward. We cannot go back to what was. What was is past, and there is only the future to focus on. When the old is gone it is gone, and we must move forward—toward new life."

She was right, as was John, and so in my "new life," I decided I would focus on creating three things.

First, the reclaimingthesky.com website—to give aviation employees an opportunity to share emotions around 9/11 and tell how they are recovering, as well as provide them with an opportunity to gain support to meet the challenges of keeping America flying during a turbulent time. That website is up and running, and recently ivillage.com contributed the software for a Message Board that will give visitors to the site an expanded opportunity to open discussions and give and get support.

Secondly, there is the issue of the "under the radar" suffering, as John called it, that is still going on with people's unresolved issues around 9/11. I aw evidence of that on my "journey," and as such I think there's an opportunity to reach out to a major research university to get the school involved with the Reclaiming the Sky Institute, the non-profit a group of us has created. The goal would be to explore the needs of aviation workers, and suggest mind/body solutions we can pass back out to the aviation industry through its various national associations.

An ambitious task, and it will take reaching out for corporate, government and private support to achieve that.

Finally, there's the issue of young people. I would like to see the stories of the brave aviation people in these pages become a base for teaching high school students about "empathy." We will create a curriculum to take the next step to teach them how to apply that empathy to their writing, to teach them how to enhance their writing skills.

Another big job, and another go round to search for the support to achieve it. But, ah, that's the beauty of the "full" circle: this teacher gets to be a teacher again.

Now as Janet Ott says and Sue affirms: what new life would you try if you knew you couldn't fail?